Culturology

Using Organizational Culture for Strategic Growth

Stephen P. Campodonico

*Dedicated to my wife Paty
and children, Stevie and Mia.*

*There's no one else I'd rather change the world with
than you!*

Contents

Section 1:
Understanding Organizational Culture

Section 2:
Using Organizational Culture for Strategic Growth

SECTION ONE

Understanding Organizational Culture

Chapter 1

Culturology is Not Anthropology

But it's All About Culture

For the past 10 years my family and I have lived in Indonesia. We've learned the local language (mostly), have learned many of the local customs and also have a fairly deep understanding of the culture. You see I studied anthropology in college. I'm fascinated by cultures. We live in an amazing mosaic full of uniqueness and diversity, which we call our world. No matter how much you study another culture, you still never fully understand it until you experience it. Even then "culture" is full of so many deep levels; it is the mystery that once unlocked allows us to understand why people do what they do.

About six years ago we had just moved to a new city in Indonesia. We met a group of young families our age who all had children. In one way or another they were all related to each other. From this group of four families we really only got to know one couple well. We thought dinner sounded like a great idea to get to know more people and make some new friends.

Since we wanted to make a good first impression, we went to a local restaurant and ordered a wide variety of Indonesian food. We planned on dinner at 4 p.m. which we thought was pretty early to eat, but they were the ones who picked the time. 4 o'clock came, and no guests; 5 o'clock, 6 o'clock, and finally 7 p.m. came and still no guests. At first we thought it was the cultural difference many of us know about: Americans value time and are usually on time, where much of the world runs on a different clock which pays less attention to being right on time. Indonesia is such a place; a place where people live on *jam karet*, or "rubber time," meaning that time is flexible, but surely even in Indonesia, three hours late for a dinner appointment was a bit extreme!

When 7 o'clock hit, we gave up hope that they were coming, so we actually had to throw out most of the food since it didn't keep well. At 8:30, we received a phone call from our friend apologizing that they were late. "Oh, it's OK," I said, but I remember thinking, *LATE! Four-and-a-half hours isn't "late;" it's <u>exceedingly</u> late.* They told us they would be over shortly. But there was one small problem; we had thrown out all of the food!

Now I hate to admit this, but I went to the dumpster and salvaged all of the food I could. I know what you're thinking, but the food was still all in the Styrofoam take-out containers. Finally, the knock on the door came and we offered a much smaller feast than we had planned. After they had come in and we said our appropriate greetings, I asked my friend if there was a misunderstanding about the time. He apologetically said no, but the problem was he had to work later than normal. The other families had come over to our neighborhood at 4 o'clock, but they were too shy to come in without him. They waited and when he said he couldn't get there on time they all went home and waited at home until he could come.

The problem wasn't that he was in charge, but that he knew us best, and the others were simply too shy to come on their own. You see, feeling shy, or "malu" as we say in Indonesian, is a very strong part of the culture. While I assume that practically no American would be four-and-a-half hours late for a dinner appointment, we also wouldn't wait on someone's doorstep and not knock because the person who knew the family the best hadn't come yet. It simply doesn't make sense to a Westerner.

The above example illustrates a kabuki dance that I call culturology, whether experienced on the dance floor in other countries, or experienced daily within our own organizations. As we delve into the study of cultures, or anthropology, we understand better how different peoples and cultures view the world differently. Some of these views are understood, while others are deep rooted assumptions about how the world works and how it should work. These worldviews color how people see the world. In some parts of the world, getting sick means that you have some type of virus or bacteria, while in other parts of the world it means that local spirits are angry with you. You can just imagine how worldview impacts how someone treats the sickness.

Just like an iceberg, most of culture is hidden under the surface, but directly impacts everything that happens on the surface. We often don't even stop to think about why we do what we do; we simply do it. In the same way there are "ethnic" cultures around the world, our organizations all have "cultures." These cultures impact every aspect of our work and along with that the future of our companies. This is the unseen aspect of the iceberg that lies underwater, out of sight, but is the foundation for everything that happens on the surface. Because of this, understanding and creating culture is one of the most strategic tools we could use in our teams and organizations succeeding.

Once while I was in Morocco and living with a local family I got sick, probably from eating fruit that had not been properly cleaned. That night it all came out, and when I get sick it's not very quiet, so it wasn't long before the whole family knew I was sick. The mother quickly jumped into action to help me. She ran off to get something...maybe medicine...the doctor's number?...a cool wash cloth? Well, it wasn't any of these. She came back with a large perfume bottle and proceeded to spray my face with very strong perfume. Guess what happened next? Well, let's just say it didn't help at all and had the opposite result for which she was hoping.

In the same way, each nation or ethnic group has a distinct culture and organizations all around the world have an organizational culture that they shape and that also shapes how they function as an organization. Organizational culture can be different from one organization to the next. Some organizational cultures may be better than others for achieving certain things, but one thing is clear; we can't escape the fact that we live in a nation with a unique culture and we also find ourselves working for or connected to organizations which also have unique cultures.

Culturology attempts to better understand organizational culture and to help organizations see how to create organizational culture for strategic growth. In the past decade organizational culture has become more widely studied and understood. A search on Google for "organizational culture" quickly yields about four million hits in less than a second. So let's say that while anthropology is the study of culture, culturology is the study of organizational culture.

In the same way someone in Morocco may spray perfume all over you when you have food poisoning, or someone in Indonesia may *not* do something because of feeling "*malu;*" there is a culture in your organization that causes people to do what they do. Culture is the bedrock that impacts every person in your organization. It's the hidden part of the iceberg that impacts everything that is visible.

While culture can be studied, so much of organizational culture is made up of invisible givens that guide decisions which are made regularly. The culture of any one organization can be drastically different from another. Branch offices of one organization can have very different cultures, different businesses in the same market can vary drastically, and different teams in the same sport can be as different as night and day, but they all have two things in common: a team culture and the desire to succeed. Their cultures may be different, and they may be successful at what they do, but as you read this book, it should become clear that culture affects everything: day-to-day operations, the future of the organization, internal and external relationships, how to solve problems and strategic planning, just to name a few. It's my premise that organizational culture is one of the best strategic tools to use in your organization to achieve your dreams.

Lenses and Worldviews

While worldview is definitely a term from anthropology, it helps us also understand organizational culture as well. The simplest way to understand worldview is that it is the way we view the world; how it works, how to respond to things and how to interpret things around us. Organizations also have a worldview based upon their culture. This causes them to view their world in a certain way that lines up with the predominant culture within their organization.

We will examine the elements of culture in later chapters, but I hope at this point we can agree that there are visible or known assumptions, but that most assumptions are unknown by our organizations and these are directly tied to your culture. Kegan and Lahey state in Harvard Business Review (2002) that, "people rarely realize they hold big assumptions because, quite simply, they accept them as reality. Often formed long ago and seldom, if ever, critically examined, big assumptions are woven into the very fabric of people's existence" (p. 47).

Let me try to explain a bit further. I'm an American of Italian descent. I grew up in California my entire life, with the exception of my undergraduate studies completed just across the border in Arizona. When I came to Indonesia a decade ago as an English teacher, Indonesians told me they could always tell where Western tourists were because they talked so loud. I was surprised! Westerners don't talk that loud!

While I was in California, I was friends with numerous Arabic families. Now when they got together and they were either excited or angry, they – not European Americans – were loud! Possibly you're of Arabic descent and a bit offended at my stereotypical statement. If so, you're right. Not that I want to offend anyone, but I do want to make a point; our culture is birthed out of our worldview and our worldview helps to further shape our culture.

In a sense, everyone is loud, or everyone may be soft spoken. It simply depends upon our definition of loud and what is normal for you. Remember, culture and worldview shapes how we view the world. When I came to Indonesia, I used to think that Americans were "normal" and that Indonesians were soft spoken. Now that I've been here for 10 years, I'd have to say that I agree with Indonesians – Americans are LOUD! That's because after being here for 10 years, my personal culture and worldview have changed, my assumptions about the world have been challenged, and some reshaped, simply because I've encountered a new culture.

In the classic story *The Wizard the Oz*, Dorothy and her band of travelers are seeking the Emerald City, but before they can enter, they need to put glasses on and not take them off as long as they are in the Emerald City. The Emerald City is amazing! Such rich tones of green like they've never seen. But do you know why the Emerald City was so...emerald? Because the lenses of the glasses were green! There wasn't really an "Emerald" City, but our realities can be influenced by a number of things, just like lenses in glasses can alter someone's view of reality.

What lenses or glasses are you wearing that you don't even realize you have on? What shades of lenses are your glasses? How does this enhance or taint your understanding of the world around you? At times we've worn the same glasses with the same lenses for so long that we don't even realize our lives are guided by culture. There are some aspects we're aware of, but there are probably more aspects we're unaware of because those shades have become our reality.

This Way or That Way?

There's more than just one way to analyze culture. When we first came to Indonesia, we spent one full year in language study where we also were studying a lot about culture. At first the learning curve was steep. We made mistakes all of the time. Once I asked a lady if she was cooking "sweet or salty mothers" since the word for mother is similar to that of sweet potatoes. My wife asked an Indonesian woman for three snakes. The lady was in shock and asked, "What are you going to do with three snakes!?!" My wife's simple answer was, "make a cake." You see, my wife mixed up the word for eggs with snakes. These were just a couple of the language mistakes we made, not counting the numerous cultural mistakes.

Many times some of the best ways to understand culture is to simply jump into a culture and begin to experience it firsthand. There's a helpful proverb for living in another culture that says, "Blessed are the flexible for they will bend and not break."

We tried many approaches to learning the culture in Indonesia. Why? It's simple; learning the culture is one of the most basic needs to live successfully in another country, and ensure you can really help people. In the same way, understanding the culture of your organization (or the culture you need to have to succeed), is one of the most basic needs to achieve the dreams you and your organization have.

Edgar Schein is a famous observer of culture. He is credited with inventing the term "corporate culture." In his writings, he discusses three different approaches to understanding organizational culture. He states that these approaches can be conflicting in their quest to understand organizational culture.

One of these approaches is the Survey Research Approach. As the name implies, this approach uses research methods, surveys and questionnaires to attempt to understand organizational culture. This allows results which are quantitative and measurable. In this approach, the surveys make it difficult to differentiate between organizational culture and climate. Schein also questions the ability of this approach to cover the, "conceptual terrain that culture deals with in human systems" (Frost, P. J., et all, 1991, p. 244).

The second approach is the Analytical Descriptive Approach. This approach also analyzes and identifies components of culture. These components are then studied to understand the organization. Schein feels that while this approach does help to give some focus and something measureable, there are some questions or weaknesses to this approach. One weakness is that this approach may not take into account every aspect of culture and may be biased in the assumptions it makes. Along with this, breaking culture into components causes culture to be fragmented and raises questions such as, "Should or could culture be fragmented? Is culture as neat as a 7-layer cake, or is it more like gado-gado and all mixed together?" (What's gado-gado? Read chapter two to find out!)

The final approach is the Ethnographical Approach. Schein (in Frost, P. J., 1991) states that, "The ethnographic approach taken from anthropology and sociology starts with the assumption that there are deeper structures and that those structures cannot be unraveled or understood without intensive and extensive observation supplemented by interview data from cultural insiders" (p. 244). While this approach seeks to deal more with the actions and day to day life of an organization, it is also difficult for someone to really understand the culture unless there are opportunities to observe all types of experiences over a long period of time. The fear with this approach is that an observer will only receive glimpses of organizational life, but these are not enough to paint a true picture of the entire organization.

Having guests wait for four-and-a-half hours simply because one person wasn't there and they were too shy to come and knock on the door by themselves didn't allow us to fully understand the cultural impact of feeling shy here in Indonesia. This is a lesson that we learn and experience regularly and serves as a reminder of what some key aspects to the Indonesian culture are. There are aspects of the Indonesian culture that we still have yet to fully understand, but because of being here 10 years, we can immediately spot mistakes that foreigners make when they arrive. For example, do you know you shouldn't really use a toothpick unless you cover your mouth up with your hand? But, it is OK to go ahead and pick your nose publicly? In Indonesia, stealing or cheating (if it is for your own good and the person you're stealing from or the teacher whose class you're in doesn't know) is OK (well sort of), and if you're caught it isn't OK. Culture is complex; it takes time and there will be mistakes, but learning culture is a must when living overseas. In the same way, understanding your organization's culture and taking steps to create a culture to help you succeed is a must if you want to achieve the dreams and goals you have for your future. DeKluyver and Pearce (2009) remind us that, "performance is linked to the strength of a company's corporate culture" (p. 42).

Culturology is not just an analytical approach that seeks quantitative results to study culture, or an ethnographic approach to understanding culture; it is a reminder that we need numerous approaches (qualitative and quantitative) to simply begin to crack the surface of understanding our organizational culture and achieving our desired culture. Culturology seeks to help us understand the strengths of both learning about current culture and understanding key elements to help create a new organizational culture to achieve our dreams.

In the next chapter we will analyze more of the elements of organizational culture and how they are intertwined.

Discussion Questions

1. How would you define organization culture?

2. What are things or principles you could learn from thinking like an anthropologist in studying your own organization's culture?

3. Share some examples you have of "cultural" stories, either from your own culture, or from your experience in other cultures; are there any parallels or helpful illustrations in approaching understanding your organization's culture?

4. What do you think your organization's culture is good at achieving?

5. What do you think your organization's culture is not good at achieving?

6. Can you identify any lenses or worldviews that your organization has which impact how things work? If so, list them and their potential impact.

7. Do you or have you ever relied on survey research methods or analytical descriptive models in your organization? What were the results? How did you use the results?

8. What do you think about the ethnographical approach? Do you agree that there are deeper structures which shape your reality? If so, how do you think you can begin to dig down to understand what these structures and beliefs are?

Chapter 2

Layer Cakes and Gado-Gado

The Depths and Webs of Organizational Culture

In Southern California, there is a great restaurant – Claim Jumpers. Anyone who's been to Claim Jumpers knows they not only have great food, but big portions...at times HUGE portions. I've never eaten dessert there simply because of the size of the desserts. A favorite was their chocolate layer cake called, "The Great Wall of Chocolate." It boasted seven layers of chocolate cake and frosting. Unbelievable!

In many ways, culture can be explained in layers. Culture exists much like an onion; when you peel off one layer, you find another, deeper layer. There are always deeper assumptions that need to surface. The deeper assumptions are the ones that we are least aware of because they've become part of our reality; to us they ARE how the world is.

One of the benefits of living in Indonesia is the food. While not every foreigner loves Indonesian food, most don't have any problems adjusting to the food, especially foods that come with peanut sauce. Gado-gado is one well-known dish. Most dictionaries translate gado-gado as Indonesian salad, and possibly it's as close to *salad* as you can get in Indonesia, but the English term salad doesn't do gado-gado justice. If you could imagine typical salad ingredients: lettuce, tomatoes, cucumbers, beans, but also tempe, tofu, a pressed rice cake, and sometimes fruit or meat all topped in peanut sauce mixed together, then you've got gado-gado. Trust me, you'll probably like it. But the use of gado-gado doesn't stop there. The word has taken on additional meaning based upon the dish.

You may have gotten a picture of gado-gado as many ingredients all mixed together and covered in peanut sauce, and basically that's what it is. Because of that, things that are mixed, especially ethnically mixed people, are sometimes called gado-gado. Our kids are a great example: I'm an American of Italian descent, my wife is from Mexico, and our kids have lived a majority of their lives in Indonesia Now that's gado-gado!

In the same way that culture has multiple layers like a layer cake, it's also incredibly mixed up and intertwined like gado-gado.

In terms of layers of culture Schein (2010) feels that there are three levels of culture. He describes these levels as artifacts, espoused beliefs and values, and basic underlying assumptions (p. 24). These levels are described as:

- Artifacts: Visible and feel-able structures and processes such as:
  o Observed behavior

These are often difficult to decipher.

- Espoused beliefs and values, including ideals, goals, values and aspirations such as:

  o Ideologies
  o Rationalizations

These may or may not be congruent with behavior and other artifacts.

- Basic underlying assumptions, which are unconscious, taken-for-granted beliefs and values

These determine behavior, perception, thought, and feeling.

These different levels (or layers) of culture help us to see the complexity of culture. The main point I hope we understand is that there's always more to culture than what is at the surface. Just like an iceberg, the deeper we go, the more we find and often times it's the deeper levels of culture which really impact our worldview and assumptions.

Think with me for a second about certain family or ethnic feuds that exist all over the world. Certain groups simply do not like each other and some physically harm each other. Why? At times the reasons are clear, but other times no one knows because, "that's just the way things have always been." Take a long drawn out family feud as an example. Both families dislike each other. They are in a continual cycle of retaliation, but if they could stop for a second and think what started the feud some people may not even know. It would take time and a lot of effort to dig deep enough to really understand the root cause of the actions that are being done today and both sides may have a different view of reality about why the feud is occurring.

While it sounds easy...it's not.

This is because even though there may be levels or layers to culture, culture is a lot more like gado-gado, or to use a dish you may be familiar with, stir fry. People's view of reality impacts the decisions they make, what actions they'll pursue, and how they'll accomplish them. Their unique view of reality is linked to assumptions which are deeply rooted in their personal, ethnic, or organizational culture. Instead of a layer system in culture, there is more of a web system which ties many different elements together, each at different positions and each slightly different from one person to the next, but having an overarching structure or shape.

What are the most widely accepted major elements, layers or ingredients in *gado-gado* that make up organizational culture? If you want to understand not just what organizational culture is, but how it works together, this list is the best place to start. Before we understand some key elements of organizational culture let's look at some definitions of organizational culture.

Organizational Culture

Organizational culture has been described by numerous authors. Some definitions may have slight differences, but to give us all a good idea of what organizational culture is, many definitions are listed below. Organizational culture has been defined as:

- Something that, "points us to phenomena that are below the surface, that are powerful in their impact but invisible and to a considerable degree unconscious. Culture is to a group what personality or character is to an individual" (Schein, E. H., 2010, p. 14).

- "A pattern of shared tacit assumptions that was learned by a group as it solved its problems of external adaptation and internal integration, that has worked well enough to be considered valid and, therefore, to be taught to new members as the correct way to perceive, think, and feel in relation to those problems" (Schein, E. H., 2009, p. 27).
- "The way things are done in the organization" (Deal & Kennedy, quoted in Driskill, G. W. & Brenton, A. L., 2011, p. 28).
- "The set of key values, assumptions, understandings, and norms that is shared by members of an organization and taught to new members as correct" (Daft, R.L., 2008, p. 422).
- "An enduring, slow-changing core attribute of organizations. Culture refers to implicit, often indiscernible aspects of organizations" (Cameron, K. S. & Quinn, R. E., 2006, p. 147).
- "A unique sense of the place that organizations generate through ways of doing and ways of communicating about the organization; reflects the shared realities and shared practices in the organization and how they create and shape organizational events" (Shockley-Zalabak, P. S., 2009, p. 47).

- "The pattern of beliefs, values, rituals, myths, and sentiments shared by the members of an organization" (Harrison, R. & Stokes, H., 1992, p. 1).

If we can understand culture, we can understand why things are done, how things are understood and how people relate to each other within an organization. I hope that you can begin to see how important organizational culture is not only in day to day life, but also in laying a foundation which allows an organization to be strategic about their future.

When you grow up in a culture, you naturally absorb and learn it, unconsciously. But when you live overseas as an adult there are endless aspects of culture that need to be learned. In Indonesia, you need to learn how to say no to a request (often without actually saying, "No"), how and when to eat at a friend's house, to use your right hand to shake hands, to eat, and give money, not to look directly in people's eyes (except in certain situations), how to cross the street, how using a third party to solve a personal problem is acceptable and appropriate, how you don't touch people's heads, don't show the bottom of your feet, and how you shouldn't sit higher than someone, that is of course unless you want to exalt yourself over them, just to name a few. In the same way there are key elements to understanding a second culture, there are also key elements to understanding organizational culture. Below are listed some elements generally considered as components of organizational culture with a deeper look at the most important elements.

Elements of Organizational Culture

The following are key elements of culture according to well-known authors and researchers:

- Beliefs, values, rituals, myths and shared sentiments (Harrison, R. & Stokes, H., 1992, p. 1).
- Mission, strategy, goals, structure, systems, processes, common language, concepts, relationships and rewards (Schein, E. H., 2009, p. 37-60).
- Values, symbols, stories, language, metaphors, artifacts, heroes, outlaws, rituals, rules, organizational communication style, history and place (Driskill, G. W. & Brenton, A. L., 2011, Ch. 4).
- Things that shape culture: corporate vision, shared values, beliefs, assumptions, past experiences, learning, leadership and communication (Kotelnikov, V., 2011).

Along with these, other known elements of culture are related to customs, rules & policies, and the actual physical environment of the organization.

For our purposes of being a culturologist, there are five main aspects of organizational culture I'd like us to look at deeper: values, stories, structures, physical signs, and assumptions.

Values

What values does your organization hold? Do these values line up with your own? What if they are different? Do you exercise a lot? Then you probably value health. Is your dining room table large? Possibly you value entertaining guests. What's your entertainment center like? Is it full of speakers, iPads, flat screens, smart phones, and the latest technology? Then you probably value entertainment, technology, and being entertained. These are all physical signs of things we value.

Now try to think of other emotional values: honesty, integrity, hard work, teamwork, being on time, creativity, or relationships, just to name a few. How do you see values like these in your organization?

Of all of the elements of culture we'll discuss, I want to spend the most time on values. Values are the glue that holds a group together. Scott, Jaffe, and Tobe (1993) call values one of our most special achievements which are the deepest and most powerful motivators of personal action (p. 22). A team could come up with a great vision, and mission, but if they lack similar values, they will never achieve their vision because values always relate into actions. Schein (2009) states that the essence of culture is jointly learned values (p. 26).

Scott, Jaffe, and Tobe (1993) state that, "the root of values is 'valor' which means strength. Values are sources of strength because they give people the power to take action. Values are deep and emotional and often difficult to change" (p. 19). If we think back to times of valor, possibly you think of medieval times, and this actually gives us great images to work with. The role of a knight – a role of honor, a respected role, a role to protect and lead a kingdom – these all display what we would call "strong" values. Values guide what we do and how we live. Values are part of the deeper layers of culture along with assumptions.

Values, if they are good, are not meant to be limited to the top leadership or to a small group, but should be felt throughout the entire organization. Driskill & Brenton (2011) state that in organizations with strong cultures, values permeate the entire organization. They go on to state that, "these elements are consistent in their support of overall values and guiding root metaphors" (p. 42). These values guide the group. Driskill & Brenton (2011) also note that, "values may be the most central cultural construct on which all other cultural elements rest" (p. 45).

In Indonesia there is a high value for community. Indonesians have a difficult time understanding how many Americans don't know everyone in their neighborhood, let alone immediate neighbors. We often see neighborhoods come together here for parties, events, and even street cleaning. Streets commonly shut down because of chairs, a stage and a large tent or canopy. It may be someone's wedding, a school event, or possibly a funeral, but often times the event takes up the entire street. You may wonder why. It's because the people don't have any space in their house so they use the only space they have – the street in front of their house. While it is an inconvenience to have to drive around the block from the other way to get to your house, or even possibly have your car pinned in your driveway for the entire day (or until the ceremony is over) people really don't seem to mind, because they value community and working together.

There's a proverb here that states, "Neighbors who are close are more important than family who are far." It basically means that being close to your neighbors is what matters. While family will always be family, if your house is being robbed, burning down, you need some eggs or you need to chase down your loose chicken, you run to your neighbor for help; you don't call your family who lives two hours away and wait for them to come and help. This further shows the value of community here. Values help create culture and culture often reinforces values. They are the foundation which culture is built upon.

Not all values are positive. For example if an organization valued getting ahead at any cost, this too would be evident in their culture. Values simply give direction to a company's actions. If success means money to a group, then they could justify using any means to succeed in getting as much money as possible. Values can also change over the course of time. If an organization was led by someone who valued efficiency and reducing costs, they could possibly allow cutting corners in production or quality. If new leaders came along who valued honesty and quality, they would change what is valued in the organization and this in turn would change the corporate culture. Even though it is hard to label values as "positive" or "negative," we could all probably agree on a number of values which are important or which are generally viewed as positive. Simply take a second and think of the type of organization you'd want to work for and the values you'd want present. I doubt many of us would list many negative values.

If we were to go back to the root word for values, *valor*, we can easily be reminded of the importance of values. To put values in another business context, DeKluyver and Pearce (2009) note that, "shared values often reinforce areas of competitive advantage" (p. 42). Having strong values, and values everyone in your organization feels passionate about are the first step in your organization laying a foundation for future success.

Stories: History and Heroes

Stories also help us understand culture. Stories are closely linked to values also. Stories are images of the things that we value. When talking to some pastors, they recounted a story that as they traveled around to different churches or seminars over a number of years they realized that a certain church often told the same stories repeatedly. A friend commented, "Man, doesn't anything new happen here? The last time we came they told the same story!" The other pastor responded, "We keep hearing that story because it's a part of who they are. We all have our stories that we tell over and over again because it helps define who we are."

Often times our stories are related to something in our history or special people we consider heroes who are used to describe more of who we are as an organization. Driskill and Brenton (2011) define stories as, "narratives that organization members tell and newcomers hear. When you hear the same story or type of story from many different individuals in an organization, it likely has cultural significance" (p. 47). Stories can also be used by leadership to help reinforce desired values. Stories give flesh to values. Through stories people can gain images of how values work out in actions and help shape the culture with needed images.

Some values we have in our staff are close relationships, working as a team and valuing everyone. This led us to realize that we had visited everyone's home area or village except one man. He was from a very remote area of East Indonesia. Our staff decided that we wanted to visit his village all together. We all saved money for over a year, looking for a good time to go. Five months ago we went on an unforgettable trip. The plane trip to his island was only two-and-a-half hours, but the drive, well let's just call it an unforgettable experience. When we were ready to come back home we left his house in the village at 8:30 a.m. We didn't get to the capital city until midnight, and it was only about 150 kilometers (or 93 miles) away! We walked, took pick-ups, small buses, ex-military trucks, and did a lot of waiting, but made it all in one piece after a fifteen-and-a-half hour trip. People along the way felt that we must have been UN workers because there would be no other reason for foreigners to go to a place like that. Our friend's family in the village (as well as the rest of the villagers) still talk about it to this day. I have heard our staff often tell people about our trip. Usually the context it is told in is to communicate something about our relationships as a staff; we value each other, even to the point that we travel to everyone's home village all together. When people asked our staff to list highlights of that year, they all shared about this trip together as one of their favorite memories.

We should also be aware that there may be stories in our organizations that we need to change. The story may or may not be considered a negative story, but its effects could still be negative. We live on an island of over five-million people and we're the only Westerners. We've tried to recruit people to come work with us but it's been very difficult. There's a problem; people are scared. There are two main stories which have caused this. The first is a long-standing story (or stories) about the native people of our island. They are known to be rough, direct and even violent. The second story is a more recent story. Only three years ago, an American was arrested for visa problems. Because of these experiences and stories, some organizations have banned their foreign workers from going to our island. We had a couple of people interested in joining us, but when they asked their superiors for permission to come work with us, they were denied, mainly because of these two stories. If there are stories which are negatively affecting your staff you need to replace them with opposing (true) stories to counteract the negative effects of the current stories.

History

Some of the best stories come from years and years ago. At times your staff may be only focused on the future and feel that the past is gone, but this is a great mistake. One of the best ways we can prepare for the future is to understand the past. We all know the saying, "those who do not learn from the past are doomed to repeat it," but I think that even those of us who try to learn from the past repeat things. While I love focusing on the future and strategy to achieve amazing results, I've learned to appreciate the value of the past.

When we first moved to Indonesia we lived in a city called Bandung. We also lived in a house that foreigners typically rented. It was walking distance to the language school we were attending and it was in a very welcoming community with abundant opportunities to learn language and culture. We soon learned that previous tenants in that house had been from England, Australia, Korea, America and Canada. Our neighbors gave us a run down on their take of the people as soon as we could understand some language. They would say things like, "People from Canada are like this, and the Koreans do this, people from England do that, but Americans usually don't." While it is a stereotype, the neighbors had classified every nationality of people who had lived in that home. It was important to know what the American reputation was because it would affect us and how we were initially received.

Driskill and Brenton (2011) note that, "History can offer great insight into persisting organizational patterns or resistance to change. It is hard to understand the current organization without grounding cultural understanding in the organization's history" (p. 54). Minimally, history is something that should be valued and honored and more likely, it is something that should be utilized in planning for the future. Whatever has happened in your organization in the past, for better or worse, has shaped who your organization is today. Many organizations look back to their founder, a possible new product which has become their top product now, a shift in the market which caused the company to refocus, opening new markets overseas, or even times there was a downturn but the company pulled through. Every aspect of your organization's past is worth understanding and possibly using in bringing change for the future, especially if your employees hold the past in high regard.

You should realize that the culture you are experiencing in your organization is the result of something that has happened in the past. Over time, your organization's culture has taken shape. This is why the story of the past is essential to understand the present. There will be clues which help point to why things are as they are and how they got there. Nanus (1992) states that history is a mental model. It is full of values and judgments, and often reflects the bias of the historian in hopes to influence today's policies (p. 27). While history is fading away, the effects of history can still impact us today. This is why it is important to understand the history of your organization. Try to see ways in which it has brought you to where you are today. How has the past impacted and developed your organization's culture, and is this culture still appropriate for today and your future?

Heroes

I find it amazing that when I ask Indonesians about their heroes, that so many point back to the first president, Sukarno. While he did help bring independence to Indonesia, his government was also responsible for killing countless numbers of people. I'm not trying to be political, but the point is that we all need heroes and we all have heroes in one way or another. While I see a leader who used excessive force, most Indonesians see a leader who brought independence. We may even overlook negative traits in a person and simply focus on the "positive" because we all need, and want, heroes. Your organization probably has some people who are considered heroes. This may be because of something they did, a steady long-term commitment, or about who they are and how they embodied the best parts of your organization, but the fact is, heroes impact how we view things today. Often we honor someone as a hero because of their values and contributions. We make people heroes who line up with our own values. Heroes embody what we want to stand for or who we want to become.

Daft (2002) even points out that heroism can be used by a leader to achieve their goals. Organizations can use heroism to align the company's purpose with, "being strong, aggressive, and effective" (p. 403). You can call it the David verses Goliath principle, but if you only have a heroic picture of Superman then you're missing the point. Having stories of heroes helps promote the values which you want to be present in your culture today and in the future.

One organization's hero was an elderly lady who volunteered daily. She came in on time, served people with a loving heart, was reliable, caring, and a motherly figure to everyone in the office. She was not only caring, but also competent. She cared for others more than herself and that made her successful. She became that organization's hero. When people talked about the qualities they valued there, she was always the first person of whom people spoke. She was a hero because she embodied the group's values. Over time heroes become legends who can impact organizations and help mold culture for years to come.

Structures: Vision, Mission, Strategy and Systems

While not all of these elements may be described as structures by many, they do all contribute to the way a company is put together and runs. I see vision and mission as part of a structure because it helps give shape and direction to the future and as well has an overall plan of where an organization is going. Along with vision and mission, strategy itself and the day to day systems can help explain more of the current organizational culture.

Vision and Mission

I chose to put vision and mission together because they are so often worked on together. Vision and mission statements are often also paired with a list of core values. The triad of vision, mission and values gives an organization a strong foundation to be on the right path at setting a needed culture to help them strategically grow and also communicates about their culture.

Nanus (1992) states that vision is, "a realistic, credible, attractive future for your organization. It is an articulation of a destination toward which your organization should aim, a future that in important ways is better, more successful, or more desirable than the present" (p. 8). Nanus goes on to share that many leaders have told him that a compelling vision was the guiding light and driving force for their organizations. Vision and mission help us to have something bigger than ourselves for which we are striving. Some organizations' vision and mission may be considered stronger or more compelling than others, but in terms of organizational culture there are two main ways vision and mission are related to culture. The first is that we can learn about the organization's culture not only through the actual vision and mission statement, but also in how they were put together. The second is how the current culture can help (or hinder) in achieving this vision. A company will need to see if the current culture can enable achieving the vision or if a new vision and mission would actually become a catalyst to analyze current culture and change needed aspects of the organization's culture to help achieve the future dreams of the organization. This opens the door for strategic growth and success.

Senge (2006) speaks of the proper way to share vision. He states that, "the practice of shared vision involves the skills of unearthing shared pictures of the future that foster genuine commitment and enrollment rather than compliance" (p. 9). He goes on to share that dictating a vision is counterproductive. Here we can see signs of a culture that works together, values others, and seeks input. Vision is only achievable through a team effort, therefore leaders need to consider not only if their vision is a compelling picture of the future, but how they create their vision and vision statement.

The Indonesian culture is not one that lends itself to a staff all taking part in a decision. Overall it is a hierarchical society where people rarely openly question the leader and simply do what they are told. Our team took three months of weekly meetings to work on our vision and mission as a team. While many teams head off to the mountains for a weekend where they bang out a vision and mission statement, keep in mind that the process may be just as important as the final product. An organization wants a vision that people believe in and are passionate about. The more ownership a staff has in things such as vision, mission and core values, the more passionate they will be about working towards achieving it.

Our process of working on team vision and mission was initially very slow because it took time to pull ideas out of our local team members. I knew that our team culture was already one in which our team knew what they should be doing and they were self-motivated, but because of the cultural issues I stated earlier, no one on our team had ever been a part of forming a team strategy, vision, mission, core values, tasks or goals. Those on our team were very capable people, but they had simply been on teams where the "leader" told them where they were going, what to do, when to do it and sometimes how to do it. This was a chance for them to learn to work as a team to create vision, mission, core values and strategy in line with their desired future for our team. It may have taken longer than what is typical or desirable, but keep in mind what the process of creating things like vision and mission statements communicate about your organizational culture. Is this the culture that you want? Is it one your staff would want? And probably most importantly, is it one that will help create genuine commitment for your organization to succeed? Cameron and Quinn (2006) actually link an organization's vision to what they call the preferred culture. Part of seeing the future, where we want to be and what we want to accomplish, also includes who we want to be. We should not only visualize success in accomplishments, economic growth, or more market share, but we should also visualize what the culture of our organization would be like in this future.

Strategy

After we get a vision of our preferred future we now need to plan how to get there. Bradford and Duncan (2000) refer to a study by Bain & Company where they found that strategy is the number one tool companies use to gain an advantage (p. 5). Ralston and Wilson (2006) define strategy as, "the means for reaching an overall objective by the end of a period" (p. 145). They go on to state that a strategy description will include a concept, programs, resources, monitoring and response, and next steps. Our strategy helps us in the day-to-day functions and keeps us focused on accomplishing our short-, mid-, and long-term goals.

Hughes and Beatty (2005) list a number of signs that an organization's culture supports strategic leadership and strategy as a learning process (p. 202). Their list is too long to share here, but I'd like to highlight some to help us gain a picture of how culture can help support strategy:

- People are conscientious about keeping others informed
- People talk about positive examples and the initiative of people
- You frequently hear things like, "try it," "faster," "collaborate" and "initiative"
- Conversations about strategy occur in both top-down and bottom-up conversations
- People readily seek and offer help to others inside and outside of their primary work groups
- There's a shared sense that everyone has some role to play in the leadership of the organization (Hughes, R. L. & Beatty, K. C., 2005, p. 202-203)

Indonesians love soccer, but they haven't been very good at the international level. For years tournaments happened between all of the neighboring Asian countries and there were high hopes, but Indonesia's team seemed to experience little success, until this year. For years foreign players have been playing in the professional soccer leagues in Indonesia. The league caps how many foreigners may play for any one team, but all of the major clubs have at least one or two foreign players. For the most part, the foreign players are considered the best players and they often post the best results at the end of the season. The national team, though, has always been comprised of Indonesians only, because you need to be Indonesian to play for the national team. However, it seems there was a strategic shift this year. The national team heavily recruited foreign players whose father or mother was Indonesian or foreign players who had married local Indonesians. Very quickly, these players became Indonesian passport holders and were thus eligible to be members of the national team, and guess what? Indonesia went to the finals this year against all of the other Asian countries and their only loss was in the final game. Strategic shifts can only happen if there is a culture to support them, but also strategic shifts may cause there to be a need for cultural shifts within organizations. In the same way strategy should regularly be evaluated and modified, organizational culture should be evaluated in light of the vision, mission, and strategy of an organization, and be modified so that it can be also used as a strategic tool in helping an organization achieve their preferred future.

Systems

When I say systems, I mean technology, structures, rules or policies and rewards. We could quickly see how these elements impact culture. How is your staff organized? How are decisions made? How are meetings handled? How are people rewarded and also how are people punished? How are resources designed, acquired, and distributed? These are all what I'll call systems within your organization. These systems can help you see more of your organization's culture and are also areas where leaders can continue to shape a desired organizational culture.

I was once a part of an organization which used time cards, but not a time clock to clock in and out at the specific time. I usually simply rounded to the nearest 5 minutes (in my favor) and wrote my time in and my time out. My boss knew I did this and didn't mind at all, at times telling me to add an extra half hour or hour to my time. In the end I'm sure that my additional minutes didn't amount to that much of an increase in pay, but as a college student any extra pocket money helped. At another organization I never clocked in and out and didn't even have set or specific office hours, but I had an expectation to put in between 40-50 hours per week. Other jobs have employees clock in and out to the exact minute. This is just a small example of how some of our policies (in this case related to time) can help show more of our organizational culture.

How are rewards handled in your organizations? Or are rewards even given? What about discipline? The frequency, type and way awards are given – or discipline is done – in an organization is another way to look at systems to better understand your organization's culture. Possibly rewards only go to the top performer of the quarter, or possibly people in top leadership seem to be the only ones recognized. It could be that rewards are only financial, or that rewards are more symbolic and not financial. Perhaps rewards are given in a more formal setting like an annual banquet, or rewards are given very casually in people's cubicles. I'd encourage you to have numerous types of rewards as well as numerous ways to present awards, but if you want to use rewards to your advantage make rewarding someone public so that it confirms the type of values or behavior that you want to see in your organization.

In one of my first jobs, I performed a number of duties such as delivery, stocking the warehouse, receiving and shipping freight, inside computer work and outside sales. I was rewarded with having my jersey (uniform shirt) retired and hung on the wall. It was fun and enjoyable and in some ways also felt a bit like a joke, but I was shocked to return to that organization twelve years later and see that my shirt was still on display exactly where it was when I left. My boss shared with me that every new employee asked about the shirt and it gave him the chance to teach the new employees of the values and work ethic that would get their shirt on, "the wall of fame."

Another aspect of your structure to look at is how departments work together. Is there a high level of communication between departments? Hughes and Beatty (2005) state that both internal and external cross-organizational relationships are very important to the success of an organization (p. 140-142). They state that, "strategic leaders create opportunities for alliances that do not form naturally because the organization's structure or the work itself militates against them" (p. 140). I've been in organizations with numerous departments. The closer we came to budget time and presenting our desired budget for the upcoming year, the clearer the boundary lines were drawn between departments with everyone vying for as large of a budget as they could get. I was only a part of that organization for three years, and budget times were the times I liked the least. I thought that since we were all a part of the same organization, we were supposed to be working together, but in budget meetings, it almost felt as if we were enemies. Part of our future success will be dependent upon departments being able to work together. The presence or lack of working across any type of organizational boundary (e.g. different departments) will be another way you can analyze your organization's culture as well as bring change to culture.

We've heard a lot about learning organizations. This is another system to examine in terms of your organization's culture. Who decides on the resources that are used? Who has access to resources? Who doesn't? Why? The whole idea of a learning organization is an organization with a *culture* of learning. Schein (2009) notes that learning is often difficult or less natural for adults. While we don't want to admit it, we all know he's right. The older we get the more set in our ways we become. Schein (2009) goes as far to encourage us to think of ways to create new stimuli in our organizations so that we will be forced (although he doesn't use this term) to open our minds and learn. This process is called *disconfirmation,* which is described as something which is felt that is unexpected and upsets our assumptions or beliefs. Schein (2009) states that this creates "survival anxiety" which will help us in learning things we need in order to "survive." If we take this further we get a picture of an organization where learning is so valued because it is viewed as essential not only for survival, but for success. In one organization I was a part of, I was pleasantly surprised when I sat in on a meeting with the top leaders. There was a guest who was visiting and it would be fair to say this person was much less qualified than the leadership team, but they still wanted to ask him some questions. As he began to answer, all of these wise leaders took out a pad of paper and a pen and started writing. They were taking notes and later discussed the notes together to see what they could learn from this person.

All of these systems are signs to help you understand your current organizational culture. These systems should be used to help serve your strategy and as well to form your desired organizational culture.

Secret Codes (Physical Signs):
Symbols and Images, Language and
Metaphors and Physical Environment

When you drive by your property, what do you see? What physical signs or images represent your organization? How do these help or hinder you from accomplishing your goals? Do they help you be recognizable, or keep you fairly invisible? Physical signs not only help us to get known, to portray a culture externally, but also communicate something internally. What we see – from our logo, letterhead, office space, and how we talk – are all important, often forgotten elements of our culture.

There are also invisible signs such as language or metaphors we use about ourselves and organizations as well as what people may use or say about us. We may have special words that we use or metaphors we rely on which will need to be taught to and learned by new employees. All of these elements work together like secret codes which help us to crack the code of understanding our organizational culture. These elements are things that possibly are not stated directly as a part of our culture, but that still communicate very clear messages about who we are and how we function.

Symbols and Images

The most common symbol or image a company has is their logo. There may actually be numerous images in your organization, but think of images for which your organization is known. For example, Nike's swoosh. As soon as people see the swoosh they know it's got to be Nike. Symbols and images portray something about our organization and impact our culture as well. Daft (2008) states that leaders often use symbols and physical artifacts to portray important values (p. 432). These images always convey some meaning and if used strategically can also communicate values.

Cameron and Quinn (2006) state that, "Among the most important changes that accompanies culture change is a change in symbols" (p. 100). Everyone values symbols or images differently, but one thing to keep in mind is that eventually people will know you by your logo or symbol. Does it communicate what you want about your organization?

When we started an English Center in Indonesia we had a friend of mine who worked for Disney design the logo. He had total freedom to create a logo related to our name and our focus. After he sent us the first draft we gave some input and made some changes. We then took the logo to the city where we were going to open the English Center and asked people in our target group (which was high school students, college aged students, and young adults) what they thought of the logo. We took their input and made another round of changes to the logo and took the final product out again. A funny thing happened; the people who we were targeting really liked it, and the people who we weren't targeting didn't. When we showed it to some people (those out of our target group) they made comments like, "It looks like a band's logo...this can't be for a school...is this for a gang? Only young people would like that!" All of these comments actually reinforced the feeling that we were on the right track with our logo. A second step we did was to ask people within our target group to describe what they thought the logo meant. There were many similarities from one person to the next in their description, and it also fit the school's vision and mission, so we adopted the "meaning" from the people we surveyed. My friend who created it actually thought of a different meaning or explanation of what the logo meant, but we could still easily use the description made by others. Since we've opened the school, 85% of our students have been between high school to young adult aged and only eight students out of over 500 have been over 35 years old.

Language and Metaphors

Most offices have a certain lingo and metaphors which they use. This language may need to be learned to fit in. Driskill and Brenton (2011) state that, "language distinguishes insiders from outsiders and thus helps define cultural boundaries" (p. 48). This language can also be used by the group to create metaphors, or figures of speech, about their relationships or the organization. We've all been a part of a group or had friends where we had inside jokes, common words that we used (or even words we created), or figures of speech we used to describe our group. Hughes and Beatty (2005) remind us that complex ideas can often be grasped more easily through metaphors (p. 63). Littleton and Foss (2008) quote Gareth Morgan who treats culture as a metaphor. Morgan views the culture of an organization as a metaphor for what it means to work for that company. The culture itself and what it believes in or stands for can become a metaphor for that group (see Littleton, S. W. & Foss, K. A., 2008, p. 253).

One common saying we have on our staff is "*Tiga saja*." This means the three "any-s;" anyone, any place, any time. For our staff we take this as meaning that we should be ready to serve anyone, any place, at any time. If we said tiga saja to other people outside of our staff they would have no idea what we are talking about. There may also be metaphors you, or your leadership, use to describe your staff or organization. Driskill and Brenton (2011) share a story of an employment agency that used the metaphor, "a pride of lions," because all of the managers were male and all of the agents who processed orders and helped customers were female. While some of us may like or dislike this metaphor, it at least helps us gain understanding of how a metaphor can communicate about our culture. I doubt it will be any time soon that the employment agency will hire a female manager. That would disrupt the pride.

Physical Environment

The places where we work tell a lot about who we are. Our physical environment communicates about our culture; try walking around your office and looking at everyone's cubicles or offices. Some people may have flowers and plants all over their shelves, family pictures everywhere, some very neat and tidy desks, and some desks where you can hardly see the desk anymore. Now begin to look at the building; is it spacious, new, old, well kept, fancy? What about the grounds? Are there sports facilities, picnic tables outside, lots of parking spaces, statues, images or signs? Think about what these communicate about your organization's culture. Schein (2010) shares stories of how companies were intentional about their physical design. One company chose an old wooden mill to communicate that they were frugal and simple. Another company considered their employees experts in their areas. They believed in autonomy. These two aspects, individual expertise and autonomy, lead them to design work spaces which had a high level of privacy. In both of these examples the intentionality of the company helped to provide a physical design which fit who they were. This didn't only communicate their culture to their staff, but also to any visitors who walked through the doors of their office.

A professor shared a story of an organization which highly valued unity and equality. They wanted to communicate that there was very little hierarchy in their staff. This was accomplished by all of the staff (including the top leadership) having very similar offices which were made with very large windows so people could see in. Internally this communicated exactly what the leadership wanted; we are all the same, we are a team and everyone is important! As time went on though, and the company had perspective clients visit and they couldn't tell who was in charge or who the boss was. Keep in mind that your physical space will communicate something. Ideally it will communicate the same values internally to your staff as it will externally to visitors.

Deep Rooted Assumptions

Very much like values, assumptions mold and shape culture and are often closely linked to our values. One of the differences of these deep rooted assumptions Is that at times we're not even aware of them. We believe these things so much that they simply become a part of our reality. To really understand these assumptions, we need to dig, and at times dig deep, to find them. I like to think of deep assumptions as the roots of the tree. They are the part that are often not seen, but impact everything else. The roots support the entire structure. If roots become dislodged, the entire structure (or tree) can tumble down.

Wikipedia notes that the record for the deepest root structure is the *Boscia albitruca* species of tree found in the Kalahari Desert. This species of tree has had their roots reach depths of 68 meters (204 feet)! In similar ways these assumptions we are talking about are very deep – so deep that we often don't even realize they exist. To really understand these assumptions, we need to dig, and dig deep. These assumptions are so important to understand because they impact our entire organization in the same way a root system provides all of the support for the tree or the fact that a majority of the iceberg is really underwater.

The hardest thing about assumptions is not only are they hard to identify, but they really do affect everything. Driskill & Brenton (2011) call assumptions the, "unconscious levels of beliefs which make the bedrock foundation of culture" (p. 120). Organizational culture is usually impacted by the local or national culture in terms of assumptions. Just think with me for a second how an American would lead a company – like an American, right? An American would not lead an organization like an Asian, unless you were someone like me who has lived in Asia for ten years, and even then I'd probably lead an organization as more of a mix between American and Asian cultures. Our culture causes us to have deep assumptions about the world. Schein (2009) reminds us that, "deeper assumptions are often difficult to decipher, yet they are the real drivers of how culture works at the operational level" (p. 62).

Schein (2009) lists a number ways assumptions impact our thinking:

- Humans and relationships: should we be dominant, symbiotic, or passive?
- The degree to which human nature is basically good or evil.
- The degree to which human nature can actually be changed.
- Are we a part of a group or community system or an individualistic system?
- Do we simply speak the truth and be "real" or do we stay quiet and simply accept things?
- How does time work? Is it linear or cyclical? Do we have to be on time, or is being late alright? Is time considered "valuable"?
- How does space and privacy work?
  (from Schein, E., 2009, p. 63-72)

I hope that as you read through this list you can begin to understand where some of your underlying assumptions are about life and how things are done. Understanding these helps us to see why certain decisions get made, how we define life, and ultimately how we form and create culture in our organization.

I hope we can see how our culture is really rooted in our assumptions and values and how these are commonly caused (or at least impacted by) our national culture and experience. This is the place where leaders need to be careful. We as leaders can miss many opportunities simply because we've made assumptions about how things should be done. Driskill & Brenton (2011) state that, "leaders can become prisoners of their own assumptions and mindsets" (p. 134). Becoming a prisoner to our assumptions will cause closed-mindedness among us as well as our staff. Leaders must continually perform self-evaluation of their values and belief system to try and break down assumptions they may have. Driskill & Brenton (2001) feel that successful global leaders, "have learned to expand their thinking by questioning assumptions about the 'right' way to conduct business...their mental models need to be challenged and even demolished" (p. 136).

We all know why Americans as a society are struggling with becoming more obese, right? Possibly the diet? Lack of exercise? A combination of both? No, the main reason an American is potentially so obese is because we eat too much cheese. Yes, you heard me right, **c-h-e-e-s-e**. You mean to tell me you didn't know that? Well I didn't either until my Indonesian friends told me that cheese was the source of obesity in America. I know what you're thinking; you don't agree, and neither do I...completely.

My last time in the US was in 2006. I walked into the local grocery store in my neighborhood. It was a nice, newer, large popular chain and I was excited to shop for all of the foods I had missed for the past four years. I was shocked that as soon as I walked through the main doors the first display was a huge open cooler full of all of the cheese sold in the store. I counted over fifty types of cheese and you know what the first thought that came to my mind was? Right, there's the main cause of American obesity. To be honest, I still don't agree with this assumption, but the point is we need to let our assumptions be challenged and actually need to be proactive about challenging them ourselves.

We need new ways to view the world so that our beliefs can be challenged. One of two things will happen; either our beliefs will change in some way, or they will be tested, but we won't change and our beliefs will become stronger, and I'd say in most cases both of these results can be good. Driskill and Brenton (2011) note that, "effective leaders learn to continually question their beliefs, assumptions, and perceptions in order to see things in unconventional ways and meet the challenge of the future head on" (p. 136).

There's no better place to start in understanding your current organizational culture than examining deeper assumptions you have. This is the place to start as well as the place to continually come back to. In our next chapter we'll begin to see how all of these elements impact every organization and create a predominating culture which guides us daily, whether we realize it or not.

Discussion Questions

1. Do you feel culture is more like layer cake, gado-gado, or both? Why? Explain.

2. How do you feel deep assumptions impact day to day life in your organization?

3. What would you say are the top five values in your organization based upon what you see or experience every day?

4. What is a value you'd desire to be present in your organization which isn't currently evident? Why?

5. What stories are told in your organization? What "cultural values" do these stories communicate?

6. Do you know your organizational history? What events stand out? How is history viewed in your organization?

7. Who are heroes in your organization?

8. Describe things about these heroes or what they did. What values are communicated by their lives or actions?

9. What is your vision and mission statement?

   Vision:

   Mission:

10. What do your vision and mission statement communicate about your organization's culture and values?

11. What does the process about how the vision and mission statement were created communicate about your organization's culture?

12. Do you feel your current organizational culture can enable you to achieve this vision? Why or why not?

13. What images or symbols are there in your organization? What do these communicate to you? To outsiders?

14.   Does your organization (or department) have any special language? If so, what is it? What are some special metaphors? What do they stand for? What values do they communicate?

15.   What are unspoken assumptions do you have in your organization about goals, values, time, people, relationships, defining success, structure or status?

16.   What does your facility communicate about you? Have visitors (outsiders) ever commented on your facilities? What do you remember thinking the first time you walked through the facilities (when you were first hired)?

Chapter 3

We All Lean One Way

Every Organization Has a Dominant Culture

It was supposed to be an international event. They estimated that 15,000 people would come. In the end over 5,000 came and that was actually quite impressive. It was to take place at an iconic focal point of the country. It combined many things we stood for: our location and the people from that area, something with a lot of people, something people could do together and something active. Two years ago Indonesia finished a huge project – the Suramadu Bridge. The bridge spans 5.5 kilometers across the Madura straight and connects the city of Surabaya (the second largest city in the country) with the island of Madura, where we happened to be located. Actually the bridge played into our strategy of why we opened up a business on Madura. We expected the bridge to not only bring new business, but also to help Madura become more modern and we wanted to be there for a part of it.

The event was the Suramadu International 10-K run, an event to draw attention to the new bridge connecting Java and Madura Island which is not only a sign of Indonesia's advancement, but also has become a very popular local tourist spot. Indonesians are incredibly proud of the fact that they have one of the longest bridges in Southeast Asia. The race wasn't really all that international. Out of over 5,000 runners, probably 15-20 were from other countries with 10 of them being a delegate from Kenya who looked like they were a running team as they finished the race before most people made it half way. Our entire staff participated in the race with most people running it and the others waiting at the finish line cheering everyone on. It is a sign of one key aspect of our organization's culture; we value building community. We feel things get accomplished best in teams. Our customers saw the pictures and heard the stories after the race and everyone commented on how great it was that we all did it together. Our staff isn't large, but we're close.

A friend of mine observed that most organizations function like a track team where there are many departments with their own specialty, but all on the same team, but that our staff was more like a basketball team, one team where everyone works closely together to accomplish goals. I thought that was a good depiction of our team. While our key team members have different roles and strengths, we run our business more as a basketball team with everyone taking part in decision making, strategic planning and day to day operations.

The main point is that our organizations will all be different. We are all in some ways similar and different, but we will still have a predominant culture. Understanding our orientation helps us to understand our culture better. Understanding our predominant culture helps us in achieving our goals, leading and recruiting staff, and being affective in our market and environment. While there are many tools to understand our organizational culture, I'd like to direct your attention to two that I've found helpful: 1) Harrison and Stokes' (1992) work on diagnosing organizational culture, and 2) Cameron and Quinn's (2006) work based on the competing values framework related to the Organizational Culture Assessment Instrument (OCAI).

Three Directional, Not Two

Before we discuss your predominating organizational culture through these two assessments, it is important to add a third element that is not normally considered. Assessments often examine the current culture and the preferred culture of an organization. The staff of a company is asked to rank current elements of culture they feel represent their organization currently and what the preferred future, or successful future rank should be for that element. This is very helpful for the leadership to see how their employees view the current state of their organization and where they feel they should be. These results can then be used to make adjustments to shift the current culture so that your organization can be more successful. While this is the norm, I feel we often miss one key aspect of the "preferred culture" column.

Jim Collins (2001) in his well-known book, *Good to Great*, gives us an image of our company as a bus and the need to get the right people in the right seat. The image is meant to show that some people in our organization may need to shift roles, especially as our organization encounters changes both internally and externally. One aspect of this image is the fact that some people on the bus need to get off. While this could be viewed in a negative light it shouldn't. I feel the best way to take these culture assessments it to consider the preferred future column in two ways: 1) the person's preferred culture for themselves to work and grow, and 2) their view of the preferred or "needed" culture for the success of the overall organization. People need to understand themselves, their likes, dislikes, strengths, weaknesses, learning styles, and their own preferred culture to help them see if their organization is a good fit for who they are and their gifts. Possibly an employee who understands your company takes the assessment and feels your company needs to become more competitive and more focused on innovation. In all honesty, this employee could feel the future of your company should go one way, but that those shifts don't line up with their own strengths. This will help leadership as well as their staff see if the current staff are the right people to have on the bus, and also in recruiting new people to get on the bus.

I once worked for an organization which underwent a transition when the top leader stepped down. I was mainly there for the length of the transition, two years. I overlapped the end of the leader who stepped down and also the beginning months of the new leader. With any new leader there will be changes, as there should be. I was already planning on moving overseas during the transition time, so after the transition was over the new leader asked if I would consider staying if I didn't go overseas. My knee jerk reaction was, "Yes, of course." It was my job. What would I do without a job? I need a job. Shortly after that meeting and reflecting on the conversation, I came to the conclusion that I wouldn't stay. It's not because there was anything "wrong" with the organization, or with the new leader. The new leader and current leadership were all great people, but the issue laid more with me and who I was. I had come to realize that the culture of the organization didn't fit me very well. It takes a lot of maturity, and even faith for an employee to realize that their organization's culture doesn't fit with their own and step down, but think about it, we only live once. Don't you want to be in a place where you enjoy what you do and how you do it?

While these assessments help organizations to understand their current culture and their needed future culture, they can also be excellent evaluation tools to help leadership and employees to see if they are a good fit with the current and future culture your organization needs to succeed.

Diagnosing Organizational Culture

Harrison and Stokes (1992) have put together a very user friendly assessment to diagnose your organizational culture. This assessment, or instrument as they call it, examines culture in terms of power, role, achievement and support. They state that, "this instrument looks at how people treat one another, what values they live by, how people are motivated to produce, and how people use power in the organization" (Harrison, R. & Stokes, H., 1992, p. 13). The four cultures are described as:

- The power-oriented organization is based on inequality of access to resources. A resource can be anything one person controls that another person wants. In the power organization at its best, leadership is based on strength, justice, and paternalistic benevolence on the part of the leader. At its worst, the power-oriented organization tends toward a rule by fear, with abuse of power for personal advantage on the part of the leaders, their friends, and their protégés.

- The role culture substitutes a system of structures and procedures for the power of the leaders. Structures and systems give protection to subordinates and stability to the organization. At its best, the role-oriented organization provides stability, justice and efficient performance. The weakness of role organizations is in the very impersonality that is its strength. These organizations operate on the assumption that people are not to be trusted, so they do not give individual autonomy or discretion to members at low levels.

- The achievement-oriented organization has been called the aligned organization because it lines people up behind a common vision or purpose. Much of the work revolves around achievement and employees making contributions willingly in response to their commitment to a shared purpose. This culture has the deficiencies and distortions brought on by its strengths. The high energy and involvement generated by achievement orientation are difficult to sustain, and organizational members are subject to burnout and disillusionment.

- The support culture may be defined as an organizational culture that is based on mutual trust between the individual and the organization. In this culture, people believe that they are valued as human beings, not just as cogs in a machine or contributors to a task. In Western societies, this culture is the least typical of the four in this assessment. It is not valued by the power- or role-oriented organizations, so it goes underground. When not balanced by a thrust for success, the pure support culture is seldom found in business; it is not results-oriented enough to enable a business to be competitive. (Harrison, R. & Stokes, H., 1992, p. 13-21).

While you may be able to quickly see the strengths and weaknesses of each culture, it's important to note that they are also very distinct. The authors note that these four cultures are only partially compatible with each other and, "the benefits of one can only be achieved at the expense of some of the benefits of the others" (Harrison, R. & Stokes, H., 1992, p. 13). Taking this assessment can help you see what your staff identifies as your primary culture as well as the culture they prefer. After you have the results of assessments like this, the best next step is to begin discussions related to your organizational culture. What are the strengths and where is there positive alignment and what are the weaknesses and some things to change? Leaders want to not only see the best way to succeed; they also need to learn what is going on with their staff and how the current direction of the company impacts them. While this tool does not cover every aspect of culture, it does provide four cultures which are different enough to provide some clear ways to define your current culture. As the authors state, "one purpose of this instrument is to get people talking and sharing about their insights about the cultures of their own organizations" (Harrison, R. & Stokes, H., 1992, p. 25). Discussion like this is one of the needed steps to strategically use organizational culture to help your company succeed.

The OCAI

Just in case you missed it OCAI stands for Organizational Cultural Assessment Instrument. It is an amazing tool to survey people in your organization to see how you line up in four different quadrants, or four primary cultures. Different than the above example, results from the OCAI will most likely be a combination of all four cultures with the strongest leaders often exhibiting high levels of all four cultural aspects in their lives. The OCAI also has employees score the current state of their organization and the preferred state. The results are scored and then are plotted on a graph showing the balance between the four dominant cultures/quadrants. The OCAI is based on the competing values framework model. There is still debate over how to define values, their relation to each other, and their impact on culture. Analyzing culture is difficult because it is such a broad topic, but Cameron and Quinn (2006) state that, "the competing values framework has been found to have a high degree of congruence with well-known and well-accepted categorical schemes that organize the way people this, their values and assumptions, and the ways they process information" (p. 33). They go on to point out evidence of the robustness of the assessment as well as the fact that the results coincide very well between believed values and the resulting predominant culture. The four predominant cultures are hierarchy, clan, adhocracy and market. The following is a picture of the quadrants and a description of each major culture.

- Hierarchy: Organizational cultures which tend towards hierarchy are characterized by a formalized and structured place to work. Procedures guide what people do. Leaders who are effective are good organizers. Maintaining a smooth running organization is important. Key values and goals for the organization are stability, predictability and efficiency. Formal rules and policies hold the organization together.

- Market: Organizations with this culture orient themselves to the external environment instead of internal issues. The focus is mainly on suppliers, customers, contractors, and regulators. Companies in this category operate mainly through monetary exchange. The major focus is to conduct transactions to create competitive advantage. The core values tend to be competitiveness and productivity. Profitability, bottom-line results, strength in market niches, stretch targets and secure customer bases are primary objectives of the organization.
- Clan: Organizational cultures with a clan culture resemble a family-type organization. Some basic assumptions in a clan culture are that the environment can be best managed through teamwork and employee development, customers are best thought of as partners, the organization is in the business of developing a humane work environment, and the major task of management is to empower employees and facilitate their participation, commitment, and loyalty. Success is defined in terms of internal climate and concern for people.
- Adhocracy: This culture seeks to foster adaptability, flexibility, and creativity where uncertainty, ambiguity, and information overload are typical. Adhocracy's root word is *ad hoc.* This culture is usually the most responsive to an increasingly changing world

that organizations are encountering today. There is a focus on developing new products and services and preparing for the future, and that the major task of management is to foster entrepreneurship, creativity and activity "on the cutting edge." It is assumed that adaptation and innovativeness lead to new resources and profitability, so emphasis is placed on creating a vision of the future, organized anarchy, and disciplined imagination. People stick their necks out and take risks. The organization's long-term emphasis is on rapid growth and acquiring new resources. (Cameron, K. S. & Quinn, R. E., 2006, p. 33-45).

The following is an example of a completed OCAI graph with the current and preferred cultures as well as a set of organizational effectiveness indicators on the outer edge of the graph. After that is an example of the competing values framework. You should be able to see how the quadrants relate to each other.

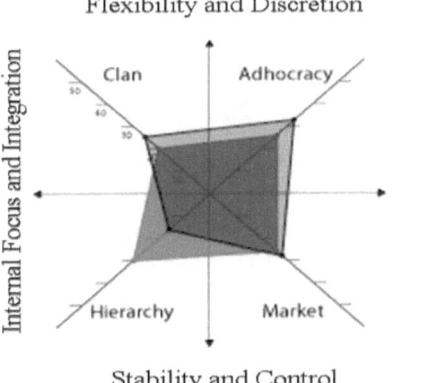

Flexibility and Discretion

Internal Focus and Integration

External Focus and Differentiation

Clan   Adhocracy

Hierarchy   Market

Stability and Control

> While the OCAI is best used with all of your employees, if you are unfamiliar with it, individuals can take it online for free at: http://ocai-online.com/

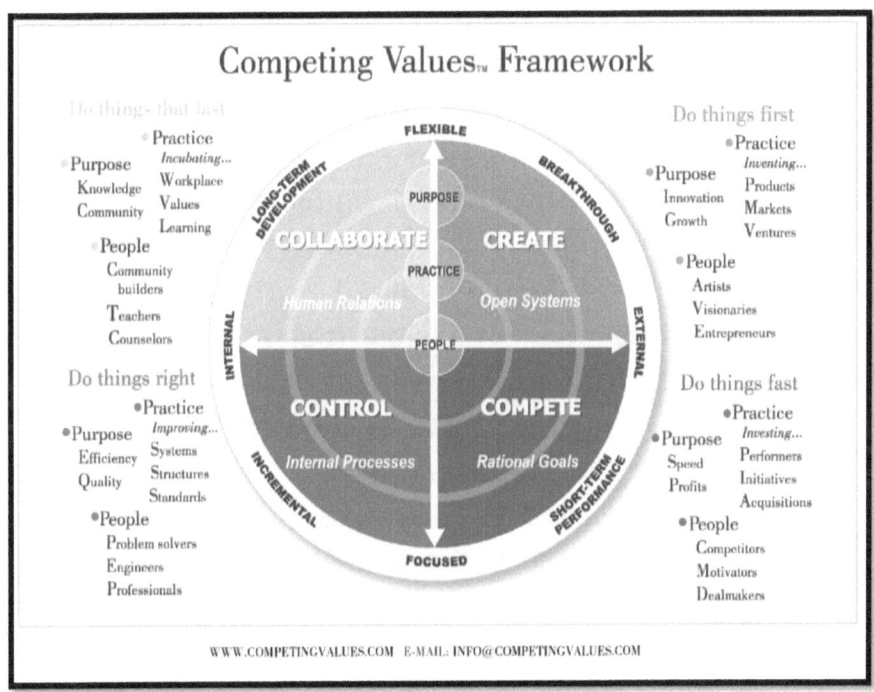

Competing Values™ Framework

Do things that last

Do things first

- Practice
  Incubating...
- Purpose
  Knowledge
  Community
  Workplace
  Values
  Learning
- People
  Community builders
  Teachers
  Counselors

- Practice
  Inventing...
- Purpose
  Innovation
  Growth
  Products
  Markets
  Ventures
- People
  Artists
  Visionaries
  Entrepreneurs

FLEXIBLE

LONG-TERM DEVELOPMENT   BREAKTHROUGH

PURPOSE

COLLABORATE   CREATE

PRACTICE

Human Relations   Open Systems

INTERNAL   EXTERNAL

PEOPLE

CONTROL   COMPETE

Internal Processes   Rational Goals

INCREMENTAL   SHORT-TERM PERFORMANCE

FOCUSED

Do things right

Do things fast

- Practice
  Improving...
- Purpose
  Efficiency
  Quality
  Systems
  Structures
  Standards
- People
  Problem solvers
  Engineers
  Professionals

- Practice
  Investing...
- Purpose
  Speed
  Profits
  Performers
  Initiatives
  Acquisitions
- People
  Competitors
  Motivators
  Dealmakers

WWW.COMPETINGVALUES.COM   E-MAIL: INFO@COMPETINGVALUES.COM

Context Matters

As the survey itself and the results are explained, please keep in mind that the survey can be contextual. There are certain factors which could impact the results of the survey. The actual context or setting of the organization can cause stronger organizational cultures to emerge. A global business with offices around the world may have dramatically different office cultures from one office to another simply based on the home culture of the country in which they are living. This could also occur with a diverse staff. If people on your staff are from different cultural backgrounds, differing belief systems, different ages, etc. the results could vary from group to group. For example in Western countries collaboration and innovation are usually highly valued. In Asian countries, control and conformity are more valued. While this is a stereotype, it is very possible that someone from a Western country could be in an Asian context and rate the "control" quadrant very high simply because the context is a more controlled context than they are used to. Likewise, someone from an Asian context could come to a Western setting and rate "collaborate" and "create" very high simply because it is much higher than they are used to in their home context.

The life cycle of an organization can cause certain cultures to emerge. For example, many start-up companies are in what some people call the "go-go" stage where all they are doing is going. In this part of their life cycle, innovation may be driving the business thus "create" may come out as a very dominant culture. As time goes on and the business sees there is a need for more rules and guidelines, a "control" culture may begin to emerge. At times a leader may be more likely to hire innovative people whereas other times a leader may be more apt to hire a controlling and regulating person because of the differing needs of the organization.

Our staff in Indonesia had very similar results when taking the OCAI. We were very dominant in the clan culture, followed by adhocracy (create), hierarchy (control), and lastly market (compete). I feel there were two main factors for our results: 1) our context and 2) our leader, or me, and the influence of the leader, which we'll look at more in chapter five. While these values are called the "competing" values framework, I do want to pause for a moment to say that although some of these values are opposing values or cultures, part of the art of leadership is for these values not to be competing, but to be collaborating or to work together.

Cameron and Quinn (2006) state that they have discovered, "That the highest performing leaders have developed capabilities and skills to allow them to succeed in each of the four quadrants. These leaders are self-contradictory leaders in the sense that they can be simultaneously hard and soft, entrepreneurial and controlled" (p. 47). In this sense the values may not be competing with one another, but can collaborate or work together with certain values or aspects of a culture to be more prominent at certain times and situations in the life cycle of an organization.

So just two questions remain – which type is your organization? And probably a more important question - What culture do you need to be to succeed?

Discussion Questions

1. What aspects of your organization's culture are a "good fit" with who you are? Why? Explain.

2. What aspects of your organization's culture are not a "good fit" with who you are? Why? Explain.

3. Based on Harrison and Stokes (1992), how would you evaluate your organization? How power oriented, role oriented, achievement oriented, or support oriented are you? What are the strengths and weaknesses of this?

4. If you haven't done so already, take the OCAI and remember to try to encourage three answers: your current culture, the preferred

culture for success, and your own preferred culture based upon your gifts and talents.

5. After you have taken the OCAI and are more familiar with it, discuss the results with your leadership team and make a plan for more people in your organization to take it. Identify who you want to take it, but remember that context could impact responses. I encourage you to include as many people as possible, especially those you may not think of: people at all levels of your organization, newly hired people, people from every department or role.

6. While people are taking it, begin to make plans how you will use the results of the OCAI in planning for your future. This is too good of a tool to simply see the results and be impressed or possibly even disagree. Use the results to not only analyze your current culture, or what culture you may need to become to succeed in the future, but also to analyze if you have the, "right people on the bus and if they are in the right seats."

Chapter 4

Curiosity Killed the Cat, but Creativity Probably Saved Him

Some Essential Aspects of Organizational Culture to Remember

Indonesia is a beautiful and lush country. There are incredible beaches, gorgeous oceans and very creative and lush gardens. If these gardens were in America, they would be equipped with the latest sprinklers, drip systems, and fertilizers. They'd be equipped with the works, but not in Indonesia. We were staying in a hotel right on the beach a couple of years ago. As we walked by beautifully groomed lawns, we saw a gardener watering the lawns. Their advanced watering system consisted of a hose and a plastic water bottle, like the water bottles you buy in the supermarket. The hose end was shoved into the plastic bottle and someone had poked holes into the bottle so that it worked perfectly like a...sprinkler. It didn't cost anything other than possibly buying a bottle of water, or finding the bottle in the trash from one of the hotel guests, but it was the most creative sprinkler system I've ever seen.

One element in organizational culture that I think deserves more attention is creativity. Too often creativity is grouped into areas such as the arts: drama, painting, acting, filmmaking, design, poetry, song, music and sculpting just to name a few, but this is a too limited definition of creativity. Creativity is also more than innovation as described in the adhocracy culture in the previous chapter. In talking about personal mastery, Senge (2006) states that achieving personal mastery (which is described as the discipline of personal growth and learning), "means approaching one's life as a creative work, living life from a creative as opposed to a reactive viewpoint" (p. 131). I firmly believe that all of us are creative. While we all may not be the best painters, sculptors, singers, or writers, we're all immensely creative in our own ways.

Daft (2008) defines creativity as, "the generation of ideas that are both novel and useful for improving efficiency and effectiveness of the organization" (p. 463). If we use this definition, creativity means coming up with good ideas which are useful in some way. It is important to understand that being creative might not mean coming up with completely *new* things, such as an invention. I feel this is just one part of creativity. Being creative could also mean thinking of a *new way* to do something or a *new use* for a product. Can you see how creativity is needed at all levels of our organizations and not just the R&D department? Creativity could help an organization to think of a new market, new strategies, and methods to cut waste, methods to increase employees' salaries or benefits, or impact the world through different social outreaches. None of these ideas deal with creating a new product, but all have to do with taking the time to be proactive about being creative.

Daft (2008) feels that most companies focused on a knowledge economy during the 1990s-2000s meaning that knowledge was the key to success, but this economy is quickly giving way to a creativity economy in our present age (p. 462). Are you preparing for your future? What role is creativity encouraged among your staff? In our world of increased change, creativity is becoming more essential for companies to gain a competitive edge.

The principle of Nine Lives

The proverb, "Curiosity killed the cat," has its origins back in the 1500s and throughout time has basically meant that it is dangerous to be too curious. While this could be true in certain situations, I can't see how it would be too dangerous in an organizational setting. There can be risks in being curious, but curiosity has to be one of the foundational elements of being creative, and I think it is actually a greater risk to not be curious than to be curious and take risks. An organization that no longer is curious is on a slippery slope of losing any competitive edge. I wonder if the reason we say cats have nine lives is that through their curiosity they were able to figure out ways to survive certain situations that most other animals (or us) would not have made it through. Have you ever seen a cat fall off a fence, out of a tree or even off the roof? Somehow they manage to twist their bodies quickly enough to land on their feet. In the amount of time it takes us to figure out what is going on they've usually maneuvered themselves to ensure their survival. Living in such a way we've defied death enough for people to say we have nine lives oozes with risk. An essential element of a creative culture is that there will be risks.

In talking about organizational risk, Driskill and Brenton (2011) note that, "Creative risks in an organization are more likely to occur in the context of members telling stories about being rewarded for such risks. Creative risk as a value in the organization is derived from the power of members talking to one another (p. 20). Taking risks could cause us to end up in more difficult situations, but those are the exact situations which force creativity in seeking a way out; just think of the Apollo 13 mission and the creativity that was needed to bring our astronauts home. Your organization will never know if you have nine lives if you don't take risks. Through taking risks you may very well find that you have many more lives than nine.

One of our efforts has been to start a private English school on a smaller island in Indonesia. Before coming, everyone we talked to warned us about coming here. The people are not friendly, the city is not easy to live in, there are no foreigners there, you'll be leaving a nice city and nice people to go where people steal, cheat, and lie. As you can image the ethnic group and island where we were planning on living was not well liked. Most people would call it risky to say the least, but we came anyway and we've had an amazing experience. We've been warmly welcomed, made great friends, found a good environment for our family, and currently have more students than we can handle at that school.

Have the Explorers All Been Lost Exploring?

Daft (2008) states that, "Most people have a natural desire to explore and create, which leads them to want to initiate creative activity in their own. Unfortunately, this desire is sometimes squelched early in life by classroom teachers who insist on strict adherence to the rules" (p. 464). It seems that the creativity and desire we had for exploration as children fades away too quickly. How many of us turned our rooms into jungles, walked around asking our parents "why" questions to the point where they became impatient and quickly answered, "Because I said so," or some other version of that timeless answer? When I was a child exploration was encouraged, but sadly the older I've become the more negative exploration seems to be. It involves too much risk, possibly goes against the norms or rules we have, and probably most importantly takes time; and we all know that time is money. Ironically we've often created worlds in our organization that start with creativity, but as growth occurs, and time goes on we move much more to sustaining and stability than we do to creating and empowering. Creativity helps us connect again to who we are at our core. Senge (2006) states that, "as the connection to 'who we are' starts to become clear, the next question arises: how a new vision can tap into the organization's creative process" (p. 305).

Cornish (2004) encourages us to be explorers of the future. Most explorers had a "productive" dreaming which helped them anticipate possible future needs so they could be prepared for them. This productive dreaming is one type of futuring (p. 7). He goes on to state that, "thinking creatively about the future (and I would add about our present) means freeing our thought processes to imagine a much wider range of possibilities than we are in the habit of doing" (Cornish, E., 2004, p. 64). One of the most basic levels of organizational creativity or idea generation is brainstorming. We've all used brainstorming. Some of us are more effective than others, but think with me about the process – we all throw out ideas about our topic of discussion eventually weeding out ideas that aren't as good. Some leaders and authors feel the first round of ideas should all be thrown out because those are the easy ideas or the ideas that everyone's already thought of. The second round of brainstorming begins to generate the ideas we want. These are the ideas that people really dig deep into their creativity to find. As I consider the entire process of brainstorming, whether the first, second, or third round ideas, I've come to realize that ideas generate ideas. Creativity drives creativity.

How many times has someone's idea helped you have an idea? Or their idea doesn't cause a new idea, but you have something helpful to add to make their idea better? Creativity generates more creativity.

Cornish (2004) refers to Michael Michalko's, a consultant on creativity, list of the methods that history's great creative geniuses have used in generating their ideas. He lists eight methods:

- Look at a problem in many different ways
- Make your thoughts visible; write them down (ex: diagrams)

- Produce a lot. Thomas Edison held 1,093 patents, still the record. (Can you name any besides the light bulb?)
- Combine things in new ways
- Force relationships
- Think in opposites
- Think metaphorically
- Prepare for the benefits of chance

(Cornish, E., 2004, p. 123-124)

Thankfully many organizations are learning the value of creativity. The science of discovery, heuristics, is now a more familiar topic in businesses. We've seen a lot of literature or studies lately devoted to white rooms, idea rooms, informal and formal methods to help employees be intentional about generating ideas, and organizations as a whole becoming "learning organizations." One of the principles of some white rooms is that people write their ideas on white boards or paper on the wall, and those ideas stay there. The next person who comes in may have an idea generated simply be seeing someone else's idea. I'll be the first to admit that some people just seem more creative than others. While this could be true, the fact remains that we're all creative in some way. The point is not just about coming up with a great idea, but helping our staff nurture a culture of creativity or idea generation so that they are encouraged to explore ideas, take risks, and be rewarded for taking those risks. The results may not always turn out as well as we hoped, but if we're going to discover great ideas we need to go through some bad ideas first.

While our staff meets together on a very regular schedule, I also ask them to fill out a monthly one page report. This is a combination work/personal report where I ask them to list things they've been learning, personal joys and struggles, progress on their work and important opportunities they've had during that month, but the question I always look at first is question #10, "List at least one new idea you've had this month." In Indonesian culture this is not as easy as it would seem because of the hierarchical society and style of leadership; most Indonesians have not been encouraged to come up with their own ideas. They are simply told what to do in helping achieve the ideas of others. Most simply feel too shy (a very strong cultural belief) to come up with an idea in fear that it will not be a good idea. If anyone on our staff has left question #10 blank, I refuse to accept their report until they have something, anything, written down. For me, it's not just about getting new ideas, although that is part of it. It's more about creating a culture where our staff is continually *thinking* of new ideas; a culture where creativity is simply a part of who we are and how we function because creativity will generate more creativity. New ideas will create newer ideas.

Ziploc® Bags and the Bigger Picture of Creativity

One of the most beautiful images of creating has to be having children. While we may have different views on the origins of humankind and if we have changed over the years or if we were created by a Higher Power, we all share one thing in common; two people (our parents) got together and created us. You may have created one, two or more lives as well. Creativity can have huge implications; with it we have the power to create life. While creativity may help our organizations start a new product line or increase efficiency in our office, the impact of our creative processes could reach much further than that.

How many of us use Ziploc® bags? If we think of storing food or kids' lunches, collectively Americans must use thousands of Ziploc® bags every day. Moreover, after we use the bags, what do we do with them? Right, we throw them away.

When we came to Indonesia 10 years ago, we weren't sure what to expect. People told us to bring many things, one of which was Ziploc® bags. Since we were going to be here four years initially we thought we should bring a lot, and we did!

While Indonesia has washing machines, driers are not widely available here. The weather is generally so hot that hanging your clothes outside on a clothes line is very practical. In our first house we had a lady who helped us with the cleaning and cooking. One day I went outside to look for a pair of shorts that I thought may still be hanging out to dry. As I went out on our roof (where the clothes were hung to dry), I noticed about 10 Ziploc® bags clipped to the wire to dry. What! This lady must not understand that once those are used you need to throw them way. Who would take the time to wash them? Not us, but since our language wasn't very good at that time we let her keep washing them. Seven years later, we were using the same bags. We still have Ziploc® bags that we have not touched since we first came to Indonesia. Just image how much cleaner the world would be if we took an extra minute or two to wash these bags and reuse them? I'm sure some of us would be too inconvenienced to take the time to wash plastic bags, but an Indonesian lady with only an elementary school education thought of a different way to do things than was the norm for me. Her creativity has helped our Ziploc® bags last over a decade. This is only one small example of how creativity or novelty could send waves of change outside the doors of our organization to the entire world. Our creativity could generate ideas that have the potential to impact societies all over the world. Who wouldn't want to be a part of that?

Don't forget, creativity helps us to connect again with who we are at our core; creators, explorers and sojourners. Organizations which can foster a culture of creativity are organizations which not only develop their people or grow their business, but could potentially transform the world. Edward

Cornish (2004) gives us timely advice stating, "Perhaps our best policy is to stop worrying whether the future will be as good as we hope or as bad as we sometimes fear and just get on with the task of creating a future that we will try to ensure is good" (p. 228).

Discussion Questions

1. How would you define creativity?

2. On a scale of 1-10 (10 being the highest) how much does leadership encourage you to be creative? _____ How does this impact your level of risk taking?

3. What are some areas you feel your organization needs to start taking some risks in?

4. Are people in your organization rewarded for taking risks? If yes, how so? If no, how do you think people should be rewarded for taking risks?

5. Do you feel protected by leadership in cases where you take risks and fail? Why or why not?

6. How is creativity and idea generation encouraged in your organization? Brainstorming? White rooms? Regular meetings or reports? What are the strengths and weaknesses of the methods your organization uses?

7. What are some ideas you have about new methods or ways to generate more ideas from those within (or outside of) your organization?

8. When was the last time you feel you risked something (personally)? It doesn't matter what happened in the end, but think about what you learned from the process. Share your experience.

9. What is one way you feel your organization could begin to take risks to ensure the future of our world could be "good" for future generations (my children and yours)?

10. LAST QUESTION - WHAT ARE YOU WAITING FOR TO START?

SECTION TWO

Creating Organizational Culture for Strategic Growth

Chapter 5

Like it or Not, Personality is Contagious

For Better or Worse, Leaders Are the Ones Who Set the Tone of Their Organizations

What if you put an entire model or engine together, but once you had worked hard, and everything looked right, you tried to start it and nothing happened? The missing piece, while only one piece of the greater whole, becomes the most important piece, because without it, nothing works.

In many ways a leader is like the one, most essential piece. While there are stories of groups of people or organizations who rally together and don't have a leader or groups who really down play the role of a leader and desire equality among all of the members, these situations are rare. In a vast majority of organizations and teams there is a leader. For better or sometimes worse, this leader is the greatest influencer an organization has.

Before we analyze the strategic role of leadership, let's look at a couple of definitions of leadership:

- Leadership is an influence relationship among leaders and followers who intend real changes and outcomes that reflect their shared purpose (Daft, R. L., 2008, p. 4).
- Leaders take charge, make things happen, dream dreams and then translate them into reality. Leaders attract the voluntary commitment of followers, energize them, and transform organizations into new entities with greater potential for survival, growth and excellence (Nanus, B., 1992, p. 10).

The leader sets the tone of the organization. Schein (2009) explains how leadership and culture are intertwined. He goes on to explain the importance of understanding the relationship between leadership and culture. Schein (2009) states, "much of the confusion about what culture and leadership mean derives from a failure to consider this interaction between them" (p. 3). Schein gives us an image of the relationship between leadership and culture explaining that leadership and culture are two sides of the same coin where one cannot be understood without the other (p. 3). We all know there are good leaders, great leaders, and sadly poor leaders, but one thing that is true of all leaders is that their lives (or we could say personal culture) will disseminate throughout the entire organization. The more that time goes on, the more our organization, team, or staff will end up looking more like us, their leader.

You've Got Five Years

I talked with my father-in-law who is an author, speaker, and leads four organizations in which 5,000+ people are involved. We discussed leaders and their influence over their staff or organization and I shared an experience where I struggled between the differences between a leader's values or culture and what I saw in the organization. My father in law quickly asked, "How long has he been there?" "Three years," I answered. "Well, he's got two more years, and after that if there are things in the organization that he doesn't like, he needs to look in the mirror." I wondered about the timing and asked, "What's magical about five years?" My father-in-law went on to explain that in his experience and perspective, a leader has about five years to influence an organization. If they've been leading less than five years, things that are "undesirable" could possibly be residual things from the previous leader (although the size and scope of the organization impacts this). However, if it's been over five years and there are things that the leader doesn't like, he or she probably needs to look in the mirror because the problem is probably not their staff, but themselves. I know that we could debate the timing and the fairness of his statement to a leader, but this has played out in my own personal experience. It helps to put a fair level of responsibility on the leaders. The more time that passes the greater level of influence the leader will have been able to have on their organization. This "five years" also doesn't mean that a leader can no longer influence their organization after five years, but that it has been long enough for a leader to address residual influences from the previous leader which need to change.

In chapter three we talked about the Organizational Culture Assessment Instrument (OCAI). I most recently worked through the OCAI with my staff last year (2010). After I got the results back, I needed to double check them. The results that our team listed were practically identical to my leadership style with clan and create being the two stronger areas, and control and compete being the less prominent areas. As they listed the current and preferred culture there was very little difference also. At that point I had been leading this particular team for five years. During those five years we had added new team members and also had to let some go, but throughout the process of working on all of the issues that we've talked about which make up organizational culture, the team's culture had aligned very closely to my own leadership style. If we think back to Jim Collins' (2001) image of getting on or off the bus and getting in the right seat, part of the leader sculpting culture will cause some people to get off the bus on their own, while some people the leader may have to ask to get off or to change seats. This does not mean that every person in the organization will be like the leader. Everyone's strengths, weaknesses, personalities, and styles are different (and we want that!), but the overall organizational culture will in many ways reflect the leader.

The Culture-Leadership Connection

Earlier I stated that leadership and culture were like two sides of the same coin. I hope this is obvious to you. Whether you rose through the ranks at your organization or were hired as the CEO from the outside, the person with the greatest potential authority and influence is the leader. How you act, dress, speak, the things you value, what you reward or look down on, will all communicate something to others in your organization and will impact the culture of your organization. Often these may be unknown or unintentional, but also try to imagine how strategic it could be if you used these things intentionally.

Years ago I taught at a local university here in Indonesia. While I was not the "leader," or even close to that position in the hierarchy of the school, I was one of the most visible and influential teachers because I was the only foreigner on staff. We often had school wide meetings where the professors would take turns speaking. While I knew that the Indonesian culture as a whole is a more formal culture than the American culture, no one had ever talked to me about any type of dress code at the university. I dressed in a way I felt was culturally polite, but also in a style that I liked. In my context, one thing this meant was *no tie*. After speaking a few times I realized that more and more professors (who usually wore ties and sports jackets when they spoke) were dressing more casually when they spoke. Although I didn't intend it, professors who were tired of wearing sports jackets and ties began to follow my lead in how they dressed. I unknowingly went against the current culture of the school that stated that anyone on the stage must wear a tie and preferably a sports jacket and I began to create a new culture, which was to look polite, but that it didn't mean you had to wear a jacket and tie.

Everything we do has the potential to impact our culture. The level of potential impact increases in line with our authority, influence, or position. Thus we're brought back to the culture-leadership connection. Who in your organization has the most potential authority or influence? Right, leaders.

Schein (2009) states that there is interplay between culture creation, reenactment, and reinforcement and that this creates, "interdependency between culture and leadership" (p. 3). Schein goes on to state that new leaders in an organization have some possible options when they encounter the organization's culture. A new leader taking over an organization can:

- Destroy the existing culture
- Fight the existing culture
- Give in to the existing culture or,
- Evolve the existing culture
  (Schein, 2009, p. 4-5).

Driskill and Brenton (2011) state that, "The leader, once he or she emerges, becomes an embodiment of the culture and has a unique fit between the leader and values of the organizational culture" (p. 186). While there are some cases where the leader went one direction and everyone else went a different direction, this is extremely rare. As leaders most often look to vision, mission and success (usually defined through financial growth) for strategic growth, I feel far too many miss the important realization that evolving or creating a needed organizational culture to accomplish these goals is one of the most strategic steps that can be done. If there is a culture which will help support the leader, the vision, and desired future, a lot will take care of itself.

Driskill and Brenton (2011) quote Beinnis (1986) who states that, "the single most important determinant of corporate culture is the behavior of the chief executive officer. He or she is the one clearly responsible for shaping the beliefs, motives, commitments and predispositions of all executives" (p. 186). Driskill & Brenton (2011) also quote Schein (1992) who went as far to state that the only thing of real importance that managers do is to create and manage culture (p. 186).

Cultural Architects

While we often think of the leader as the captain of the ship steering the ship the way that they need to go, it is not a complete picture. In many ways a leader is also like an architect. The architect is really in charge of the design of the building and at times making sure the construction happens properly. In the same way, leaders are in charge of designing the day-to- day life, future focus, and culture of the organization or team they are leading. Their decisions and actions are what help the organization or team form and develop into what it will become in the future. There are a variety of direct and indirect tools that leaders can use in becoming cultural architects. Driskill and Brenton (2011) state that, "leaders can create the conditions for cultural change by embracing and modeling new values and assumptions, interacting with and listening to employees, and responding appropriately to resistance to change" (p. 186-187).

For those of you who are married, or possibly have a very close friend who knows you better than anyone else, let me ask a question, "Have they ever completed a sentence you were saying?" Or possibly they knew what you were going to say before you even said it. These are simple examples about how we learn from each other, how people know what we stand for, our values, even down to our own thoughts, and at times they know them even before we do.

At a very deep level this is how a leader can impact organizational culture. Choosing the right values, styles, and interactions can be the key to your future success. While it is your employees who will actually help you succeed, the right culture is one of the strongest guiding forces in your employees achieving the desired future for your organization. Creating culture takes time, effort, and maintenance, but it can be accomplished. Adamchik (2006) reminds us of this noting that, "Organizational culture is not a self-sustaining process. Leaders become the stewards of the culture" (p. 167). Remember, leaders are not just the captains of the ship; they are also the lead architects.

Commander's Intent

There's a principle in many leadership books today which is rooted in the military called commander's intent. While I've read about it in books and popular literature, I love to talk about it with people who are in or once served in the military. Their stories and experiences seem to paint the best illustrations of commander's intent. Wikipedia defines commander's intent as:

> In mission-type tactics, the military commander gives their subordinate leaders a clearly defined goal (the mission), the forces needed to accomplish that goal and a time frame within which the goal must be reached. The subordinate leaders then implement the order independently. The subordinate leader is given, to a large extent, the planning initiative and a freedom in execution which allows a high-degree of flexibility at the Operational and Tactical levels of command. Mission-type Orders free the higher leadership from tactical details. (http://en.wikipedia.org/wiki/Commander%27s_intent)

Wally Adamchik (2006), US Marine and currently a speaker and consultant, describes the necessity of commander's intent stating:

Everyone must know the intent of the action, the overall objective of the engagement they are involved in, and basically how it will be accomplished. Often in combat, leaders in the chain of command are unable to exercise command, either because of casualty, a communications failure or the fog of war – that natural confusion resulting from the chaos of combat. In any of these situations, commanders' intent makes sure that everyone in the unit knows the objective and is able to move towards it." (p. 137-138).

Commander's intent helps everyone know from the leader where they are going, what needs to be accomplished and how they are a part of it. Having the right organizational culture will also create an environment where things like commander's intent (although possibly not this actual term) are understood and a part of everyday life. It is a reflection of the leader and the culture that they helped establish and reinforce.

One of our values at a school we ran was that we would try everything we could to help young children attend our school even if they did not have the financial resources. While I was gone for some training, we had a new group of children come to attend one of our clubs, but they couldn't pay. Our team worked together to find a way to cover the costs of the group and now these children regularly attend that particular English club. When I returned, they told me what had happened and how they came to their decision which is exactly what I would have suggested for them to do had I been there. Once a leader creates a foundation of a clear organizational culture, many natural processes in the day to day function of the organization will happen automatically because there will be clarity, value and purpose for the employees.

Back to the Architect

It is not enough for a leader to lay a strong foundation in creating and molding the needed culture in their organization, but there is a lot of fine-tuning which needs to be constantly done.

As general organizational culture emerges and takes root, it will also encounter different cultures – the personal cultures of your employees. While this isn't necessarily a bad thing, it is something leaders need to keep in mind. Your organization is made up of potentially thousands of people, all with their own unique views, values, and experiences which lead to their own deep rooted assumptions. The organizational culture you are trying to create could fit perfectly with their personality, or it may encounter some resistance. This is why a leader must keep in mind that probably one of the most essential tools in communication culture is dialogue. There has to be an open and constant channel of communication where anything the leader says or does is in line with the organizational culture they are trying to establish and affirm.

Driskill and Brenton (2011) list some helpful ways for leaders to communicate: recognize that all actions and statements will convey cultural significance, tell stories, capitalize on the significance of rituals, understand the value of historical continuity, use language to shape meaning and values, recognize identification with organizational values as a form of unobtrusive control of employee behavior, and demonstrate optimal competence by demonstrating the ability to take multiple points of view on the organizational culture (p. 189 -195). Schein (1992) feels that there are four ways leaders transmit culture: 1) by what they pay attention to, measure, and control; 2) by their reactions to critical incidents and crises; 3) by deliberate role modeling, coaching, and teaching; 4) by their choice of criteria for recruitment, selection, promotion, retirement, and "excommunication."

Just think of the missed opportunities we as leaders have had over the years! Every single thing we do (or don't do) in some way impacts culture, and the only way we will help create the needed organizational culture is by being intentional about the areas listed above. You are not just the captain of the ship; you are really more than that. You are more like the designer of the ship just like an architect is in charge of designing the plan to reach a final product. You are the designer not just of the actual ship, but also of the ambiance, the "feel" of the ship when people walk on, the way guests are served, the way your employees look, and the way people treat others. As you dialogue with your leadership teams, managers, staff, and departments, think of what you want to communicate first, not just the message, but what the message will bring with it (or how you communicate it); this is when we focus on not only completing a task, but on crafting organizational culture.

Another example to help us see how behavior impacts more than a written list of "do's and don'ts" is to think of a parent and child relationship. Children who still live with their parents (and even those who don't) see their parents in a number of situations, including direct and indirect communication. The other day I caught my son scolding his younger sister for doing something she shouldn't have been doing, but what was interesting was that he was using practically the same language, body position and movements as I have used in the past with him and my daughter. It's not as hard as you think to communicate values because it is actually a part of everything we do. What is hard is to correct and change your organization's culture if it's already been established. The more change you feel your organizational culture needs, the more intentional you need to be to communicate through every means possible what the new culture should be like and why.

We had entrusted one of our teams into the hands of a very capable man who I knew well, but our working relationship was somewhat new. He led one of our teams at a language center in my absence for the first six months. Even though our staff had talked through a list of values, our vision and mission, as well as a simple code of conduct, when he moved to the new location for our language center with the staff, his true colors came out.

The man who was handling the staff and the new language center was a very strong task leader even though we had formed the team in a more socio-emotional style. This style of leadership reflects my leadership style more, but also what the team felt helped us in being more strategic in prioritizing our students and our future growth. Once the staff was on their own and the direction changed to a more task and results oriented culture you can image how the staff felt, especially since they preferred the way things were. After I resumed leadership of the language center it took time to change the culture back to where it was before they had moved, but we looked for every opportunity to show that finances and the bottom line weren't all we were concerned about. We were concerned about our students and through this we felt our language center would grow.

This meant that we went out of our way to lower prices, give discounts, repay money when available, spend time with students, build community, and value the students' input in helping to bring change to our center. After a few months of changes, the man who led the team for six months stepped down. I think it's obvious why. As a leader, there will be a continual need to reinforce your desired culture so that it can continue to evolve. As your organizational culture is actively managed and led (not only by you, but through others as well – remember commander's intent), the culture will begin to work its magic through being one of your most effective strategic tools in achieving your dreams.

Reinforce, Reinforce and Reinforce Again

I once had a US History teacher in high school who said, "if I say something once it could be important, if I say something twice it's probably pretty important, but if I say something three times (or more) you'd better write it down because it'll be on your test!" One of the greatest things that leaders can and need to do in creating their desired culture is to reinforce. To put it simply, reinforce everything you desire in your culture and don't reinforce (at all!) anything you don't want in your culture. There are many ways to reinforce values or actions which you want to espouse in your organization's culture. How you live, speak, and act throughout the day will be the greatest reinforcement to the culture you desire. Remember the five year principle? Your life is a model for others. They will most naturally follow your lead.

But not everyone will be able to see your actions, or hear everything, especially if you are a part of a larger organization. This is where you need to also teach, coach and release.

When I say release I mean that there may be times you cannot even reach all of your employees through teaching. This is when you need to teach through the ranks. While you should do everything you can to have some level of contact with everyone, in cases where you can't, you can still teach through your senior and junior staff so that the principles and values you desire are still being taught all the way down the ladder. You must find trustworthy people and release them to bring the message to others. Moreover, after you release, you must reinforce things you want in your organization. You must champion all of the things you'll need to help you, your people, and ultimately your organization to succeed.

These things will help to create the right condition in an organization to develop a desired culture. An often underused method of reinforcement is rewards. Rewards come in all shapes and sizes, but most often in the form of some sort of bonus, raise or even a promotion. Rewards in this sense are reinforcement that the person has done a good job. In the same way we reinforce hard work we can also reinforce desired aspects of organizational culture through rewards. Schein (2010) gives an example that, "if the goal of a change program is to learn how to be more of a team player, the reward system must be group oriented, the discipline system must punish individually aggressive selfish behavior, and the organizational structures must make it possible to work as a team" (p. 307). Rewards aren't just about promotions and aren't just financial, rewards are about acknowledging something that you want to reinforce and want to see more often in your organization. Rewards can be very creative. One thing that rewards should always be is memorable. This could be through including someone on a leadership team, allowing them to market a new product, or coming up with a "funny" award, but making a very big deal about it for the specific purpose of reinforcing a behavior or decision that is in line with the desired culture you are promoting. These "funny" awards could be an item that has come to hold value or represents something special in your organization. As a leader you hold power to choose who receives these awards, and also when and how to present them.

It is similar to experiences we've had with our children. Often we spend what feels like way too much time disciplining them for things they've done wrong. We also should try to "catch" them doing things right. Once I peeked through the door into my son and daughter's room. I saw my son (who's older) tell my daughter, "Mia, you shouldn't do that, daddy already asked us not to do that." After this, she did it anyway. He didn't get mad that she didn't listen, but he told her again, "Mia, daddy told us to play with these toys like this," and then he went on to demonstrate how to use the toys right. At that point I burst into the room and said, "What's going on?" Mia sort of hid her face, but I went straight to my son, Stevie, and said, "Son, I saw what you did." He started to explain that he didn't do anything wrong. I then called everyone together and told them how Stevie had made me so proud because I saw what he did and what he had told Mia. This was a surprise to Stevie. I announced that we'd walk down to the corner store and pick out treats for everyone, but Stevie was in charge of all of the decisions. For a seven-year-old boy, that's pretty cool. Some of the most memorable reinforcements come through rewards or "catching" our employees doing the right thing opposed to correcting them for what they may be doing wrong.

Through rewarding properly, we also show people what we're passionate about. If we go out of our way to reward publically, we also show how we are excited by the choices or attitude of the recognized employee(s). As a leader we should passionately champion our staff and their actions when they reinforce our desired organizational culture. Shockley-Zalabak (2009) states that, "Transformational leaders are creative, interactive, visionary, empowering, and passionate" (p. 227) I think we'd all want to be described like this, don't you?

Osmosis Leadership – Values Transmission

We're all familiar with the process of osmosis. Values transmit from a leader in the same way osmosis happens. Wikipedia defines osmosis as,

> "Osmosis is the movement of water molecules through a selectively-permeable membrane down a water potential gradient.[1] More specifically, it is the movement of water across a selectively permeable membrane from an area of high water potential (low solute concentration) to an area of low water potential (high solute concentration). It may also be used to describe a physical process in which any solvent moves, without input of energy, across a semi-permeable membrane (permeable to the solvent, but not the solute) separating two solutions of different concentrations.[2] Osmosis releases energy, and can be made to do work,[3] but is a passive process, like diffusion" (http://en.wikipedia.org/wiki/Osmosis).

Osmosis is a process that just happens when there's a different level or concentration of water (solvent or liquid) on one side of a membrane. It's a passive process, doesn't involve the "input of energy," and moves from high to low. While there are plenty of issues that leaders need to actively promote in creating their desired organizational culture, the personal values of a leader happen more like osmosis. A leader can say many great things, but actions speak louder than words and these are the things that people inside, and often outside, your organization will notice. Values often take no energy to communicate since they are seen through a leader's words and actions; it's often a passive process.

Values also move from high to low, meaning that leader's values are often seen lived out in the lives of their employees. If there's a leader who doesn't have a problem cutting corners to save a buck, employees will often cut corners. If we were to take that example and turn it around, we would see the impact of a leader's, not an employee's, values. If an employee didn't have a problem cutting corners, but their boss did, and their boss found out, it probably wouldn't influence their boss to do anything except reprimand them or possibly even fire them. While much of leadership is an active process, there are also many aspects which are passive, such as the transmission of values and the way this can impact our organization's culture. In one way or another leaders model their values every day through their words and actions.

The passive side of this process is what I call osmosis leadership. Like it or not, your values and priorities will become evident and will transfer to the rest of your employees. Good and bad values will transfer. When I was young I often remember my dad biting his finger nails and telling me, "this is a bad habit, make sure you don't do it." Guess what? I bite mine too. Leaders need to pay a lot closer attention to their actions and words because the values they represent will be values that are transferred to the organization.

Leaders – Learning and Legacy

Whatever change you want to bring needs to ultimately start and end with you, the leader. We must first be willing to change, learn, and lead in such a way others will want to follow. We have read a lot in the popular press in the past decade about leaders and organizations that learn. While I don't know for sure all of the reasons, I think one reason for seeing this more in the past decade is that possibly some leaders have a slight problem...learning. Not meaning that leaders are not smart or competent, but if we look at leadership theories throughout time, in many cases the leader was never to be questioned. This is still the culture in many organizations and countries today, but what if the leader is wrong?

Our friend's son was sick. He was still young, about two or three years old, but already walking. While the medical care in Indonesia is often not ideal, if you get sick, you have no other choice. When we first came to Indonesia someone told us, "Just pray you never break a bone here because it will probably never be fixed correctly." So let's just say that good medical care is not something for which Indonesia is known. Our friends brought their son to the doctor and after the medication he gave them didn't seem to help, they went to the hospital. Their son was admitted for a couple of days. Four doctors checked him; one senior doctor and three other doctors who were all at about the same seniority, but definitely at a lower level than the senior doctor. One problem they were trying to figure out was why the boy didn't want to walk. When asked to stand up, his legs would just give way and he'd sit. When there's a problem with the legs here, the first thought is polio. The three doctors (who also happened to be medical school classmates) discussed the boy's condition and came to the conclusion that it wasn't polio, but there was one problem – the senior doctor (who also happened to be their professor from medical school), felt it was polio. Because he was the senior doctor and their professor, they couldn't disagree with him. The parents were left with very few choices as the doctor wanted to proceed as if it were polio. We were frantically reading our medical books and online medical sites to look for information about polio and from everything we read it didn't seem like polio. Since the senior doctor wouldn't change his diagnosis, and the parents felt what we were telling them was true, they discharged their son the next day after a severe warning and scolding from the doctor. Two days later he was up and moving around like normal and regaining his strength. He didn't have polio. He probably just didn't want to stand because his body was achy and hurting. What do you do when the leader is wrong? What do you do when the leader's choices may hurt others?

For leaders to really understand their organizational culture and be able to influence or change their organizational culture, they must take a learner's posture as well as help their organization become a learning organization.

Peter Senge (2006) calls a learning organization one where, "people continually expand their capacity to create the results they truly desire, where new and expansive patterns of thinking are nurtured, where collective aspiration is set free, and where people are continually learning how to learn together" (p. 3). One assumption is that a learning organization would be led by a leader who is a learner. If we combined this concept of a learning organization with what Jim Collins (2001) calls level 5 leadership, we have the perfect leadership posture to create an amazing organizational culture, one that not only helps you achieve your dreams, but one that will impact many lives, especially the lives of your employees. Collins (2001) states that level 5 leaders, "build enduring greatness through a paradoxical blend of personal humility and professional will. Level 5 leaders channel their ego needs away from themselves and into the larger goal of building a great company. They are incredibly ambitious, but their ambition is first and foremost for the institution, not themselves" (p. 20-21). Schein (2010) goes on to state that, "The culture creation leader therefore needs persistence and patience, yet as a learner must be flexible and ready to change" (p. 374). When we combine learning leaders and learning organizations we are moving quickly to another "L" – legacy.

The older we get, the more we think about our legacy. I'm guessing, but I doubt many young leaders or workers in their twenties or thirties are thinking much about their legacy, or what they'll leave behind in their organization. At the same time, I'd be willing to bet that many more leaders or workers in their fifties and sixties are thinking about their legacy. It seems the closer we get to the end of life, or the more we understand our mortality, the more we want our life to have mattered; to have counted for something. One of the reasons to create an ideal organizational culture is not just to succeed financially or gain more of the market share, but to leave a legacy, something that will outlast you in your organization as well as in others you've worked with. Hughes and Beatty (2005) talk about a leader's legacy asking some questions:

- What do you want to be your leadership legacy to others?

- What do you want others to say about your leadership after you've left your current position or the organization?
- What lasting impact do you want to have – not just on the organization but also on the people around you?
  (p. 221).

When we talk about our legacy, we're moving beyond just success in business, but talking more about success in life. One of the best ways you can create a legacy in your organization is to create a culture that supports change and develops people while it also helps your organization succeed. Remember you are the cultural architect. Look at your organization; do you like what you see? How long have you been leading? If it's been more than five years and there are things you don't like, you possibly need to also look in the mirror. Change is never easy, and often slow, but if you're reading this and you are a leader in your organization, you hold a unique set of keys to unlock the potential of creating an organizational culture which can help you achieve the legacies in life that we all desire. While no one's perfect, if you've been hired or placed in a leadership role then you have great power. And to quote Spiderman, "With great power comes great responsibility."

Discussion Questions

1. How long have you been leading your organization, department, or team? Do you think this has been long enough to bring needed change? Why or why not?

2. Who would you say are the most influential people in your organization? Why are they influential? In what areas are they influential?

3. What would be your "Top 5" list of things that you feel need to be changed in your organization?

4. Where is your own sphere of influence? How can that be used to impact your organization's culture? (Especially in response to the OCAI results & discussion).

5. What is your commanders' (or leader's) intent? Can you clearly state it? Does everyone know what role they play in helping achieve the desired goals?

6. What things do you need to do a better job reinforcing in your organization? What things do you need to stop accepting/reinforcing (or have a funeral for)?

7. What is rewarded in your organization? How are rewards done in your organization? What are creative ways that rewards could be used?

8. Try to "catch" someone this week doing something to reinforce a value or aspect of your desired culture. Think of a creative way you could publicly reward them and use the opportunity to reinforce your desired culture.

9. What are you passing on as an osmosis leader? Be honest with yourself and list out the values you may have passed on to people in your organization in the past week. Also ask five people around you to rate you on what your actions said about your values last week (and affirm you desire their honesty with no risk of consequences from difficult answers). What did people say?

10. Write out what legacy you'd like to leave your organization. Are you acting in such a way now that you could potentially achieve that legacy? What changes do you need to start making now?

11. Imagine that you're at the point in life that you are retiring. Your company is throwing a retirement party for you.

Everyone's coming and they've all been asked to write down ways you've touched people's lives or the "life" of the organization. Use the rest of this page to creatively list things that you'd like your staff, employees, board, or customers to say about you, your values, and the way you impacted people and your organization. At the bottom make a list of things you need to start doing (or stop doing) so those things can be said about you.

Chapter 6

Even Superman Needed the Justice League

The Necessity of Team in Building a Dynamic Organizational Culture

Last week I was reading a story to my kids – *The Attack of the Robot.* I know it probably will never make it on your personal reading list, but it showed me the essence of what this chapter is about.   It's a story of the "Super Friends" – Superman, Batman, Green Lantern, Aquaman and the Flash. While I'm partial to the Flash, we all know that the leader is really (and always has been) Superman. Superman has actually been caught by Lex Luthor who was inside a giant robot. How could even the largest and strongest robot capture Superman? You may have guessed; he had a huge kryptonite hand. Batman just happened to be driving by the scene and sees Superman struggling for freedom from the robot. He quickly calls the super friends to come and help, which they do, and of course, they quickly defeated the robot, freed Superman, and caught Lex Luthor. Superman finally gets free and says, "Thanks Super friends, I couldn't have done it without you." While only a children's story, there are a lot of lessons for those of us in leadership, mainly the importance of a team. How often do leaders act like a Super-man (or woman), whether that be working on your own, not being open to outside ideas, or trying to make all major decisions without team input? We have to realize that isolated leaders like this also create a culture just as much as leaders who are very team oriented.

How many movies have we seen about an obscure team or group of people who come together and form a unique chemistry which allows them to overcome, accomplish and succeed in ways they shouldn't be able to? I love these underdog stories. There's always a part of our spirit which wants to be a part of something like that. We want to go into battle with William Wallace in *Braveheart*, or better yet, we want to be William Wallace. We don't just want to "win" or achieve great things, but most people also want to be a part of something, call it a team, a close knit family, or a community. We all envy people or teams who have a great dynamic working relationship, especially when they also achieve great things.

In terms of effective culture for your organization, I like to think of the old idiom, "The more the merrier." In this chapter we'll focus on the impact of team on creating culture.

Three Layers of Merriness

While the point of this chapter is an easy one – you need others to help create your desired organizational culture – it's not always an easy reality. In many ways it goes back to what we talked about in chapter five; so much starts with the leader, but if you have the right team, they can carry things from there. While teams come in many shapes, sizes, and structures, I'd like to paint three broad stokes in images of the relationship between a leader and teams: single fighters, a select group, and KB.

Single Fighters

While it is becoming less common, there are still many leaders who seem to take a superman mentality in leading. They are like single fighters; relying on others as needed, but in the end relying mostly on themselves. This also could be the case in a charismatic leadership style where the employees place all of their hopes in a strong, but solo leader. Historically this may be rooted in the theory of "Great Man" leadership where leaders were believed to be born with certain heroic traits and natural abilities of power and influence to help them become effective leaders (Daft, R. L., 2008, p. 20). Hopefully you don't work for an organization like this. While there are great leaders, leaders rarely reach greatness alone, but we're all prone to use our authority and forget the benefits of including others. In the same way a parent may answer their child's question of "Why?" with, "Because I told you so," many leaders approach their employees and decisions with a "Because I said so" attitude. Daft also points out that a shift from the Great Man theory of leadership to more team and change oriented leadership demonstrates a trend to a "larger world" (p. 23). Shifting to more of a team based approach expands our world because it naturally includes others.

Single fighter leadership may not even be one leader distanced from, but influencing their staff. This could also be an executive board or lead team which functions as a single fighter not including people from a broad scope within the organization. This is still not optimal, and can potentially be disastrous.

Levy explains the "Nut Island Effect" in the Harvard Business Review on Culture and Change (2002). The Nut Island Effect is an organizational dynamic that happens based upon the Nut Island sewage treatment plant in Quincy, Massachusetts, which was responsible for cleaning water in Boston Harbor. Levy describes this "effect" as having a competent team which is not supported by the senior leadership and eventually becomes too independent and seclusive after their requests for help go denied or ignored. This process is more like a slow leak, but in the end is an unstoppable gush of problems, which in the case of this story led to the release of 3.7 billion gallons of raw sewage into Boston Harbor. The team at the Nut Island facility tried to get support from top leadership for repairs and needed maintenance, but because of their requests being overlooked, they had to improvise to keep the plant running. Since the plant was running well, the senior leadership felt there were no problems. If it isn't broken, don't fix it, right? Eventually the plant and the team working there were ignored long enough that the plant's four giant diesel engines shut down, resulting in an environmental disaster.

People often say that an organization's greatest resource is its people. When the senior leadership ignores those within their organization and has a solo or single fighter mentality it is practically impossible for an organization to succeed and reach their full potential. As in the case of Nut Island, not building a team culture could even be disastrous. While we know the saying, "There's no I in team," there are the letters to spell "me" in team; meaning that we all want to be part of a good, strong team.

A Select Group

I've played soccer my whole life. While I grew up playing in the recreational leagues, when I was in 5th grade I decided to try out for the city's select team. This was the highest level team in my city which traveled to other cities to play. We represented our city in tournaments and eventually entered a statewide tournament every year. Most of the guys on the team had already been on the select team for a number of years. I had missed the window of when boys usually joined the select teams, but I decided to try anyway. The way our city's select teams worked was that there was an "A" team and a "B" team for each age level. In case you're wondering, the A team is the better of the two. My friends felt I was a decent player, but they weren't sure I could make either team. I remember one friend saying, "Steve I think you should be happy and thankful *if* you make the B team." Some friend! The tryouts came and went and I got a call from the head of the organization and he informed me that I had been selected to join the A team! I was so excited, not just because I made the best team, but also because I had felt that I probably would make the B team at best. I had made the most select team, the top team, for my age group in our entire city. It sure felt good telling my friend the next day that I had made the A team when he had made the B team.

We all want to be part of a team, and often leaders do well forming certain types of teams. This could be a senior leadership team, an advisory panel, or some group of people which the main leader looks to in making decisions, communicating to the organization, and to help make sure things get done. In the same way a leader will not always be right, a team will not always be great. There could be teams within your organization which produce very little results or are more of a drain on the leadership than they are worth. Let's just assume that just like in sports, in organizations there are bad teams as well. I want to use this space to think of how having a good team can help you in developing organizational culture.

Daft (2008) states that, "to be effective team leaders, people have to be willing to change themselves, to step outside their comfort zone and let go of many of the assumptions that have guided their behavior in the past" (p. 307). It's not easy for many leaders to work with and lead teams. Senge (2006) refers to Harvard's Chris Argysis who argues that, "most managers find collective inquiry inherently threatening" (p. 25). Some leaders work easier in a team structure while others struggle. The larger or more diverse the team, the greater the challenge for the leader, but studies have shown that overall leadership teams help develop a better competitive edge than single leaders. Daft also (2008) notes that,

"A team provides diverse aptitudes and skills to deal with complex organizational situations. Many researchers believe that configuration of the top leadership team to be more important for organizational success than the characteristics of a single CEO. For example, the size, diversity, attitudes, and skills of the team affect patterns of communication and collaboration, which in turn, affect company performance" (p. 412).

Or in other words, a well formed team affects organizational culture which in turn affects organizational performance. As teams can move into alignment, their effectiveness grows. The way a leader forms and leads a team is a microcosm of how they will lead the company. The way those on a leadership team interact with each other is often a microcosm of how people will interact with others in the company. To put it in our context, every team develops a culture. The culture of your leadership team will filter down throughout the organization and create, mold and shape your organization's culture. Having high quality people on your leadership team is a necessity in forming a strong, high quality organizational culture. While this select group of leaders is a step in the right direction, it is still not optimal for creating your desired organizational culture. Including people from all backgrounds, capabilities and levels of your organization is the next step in strategically using teams to develop your desired culture.

KB

There's a play on letters in Indonesian with "KB." Originally it meant, *"keluarga berencana,"* which means a planned family and is their promotion of the main family planning motto, *"dua cukup,"* or two is enough (meaning two children is enough). Using the initials KB has also been playfully attached to the term, *"keluarga besar,"* which means extended family because if we simply add the word *"yang"* (meaning which) in the middle we have, "a family which is large," exactly the opposite message of the family planning program's message of two children being enough.

Keluarga besar gives us a good image for ways that leaders can take full advantage of using teams in their organizations. While certain organizations function more like a family than others, the fact remains that you have numerous employees or co-workers who spend a bulk of their weekly hours together performing a variety of tasks to achieve one major goal; to help your organization succeed. In this sense the more the merrier applies. The more alignment there is in your organization between the overall vision and goals, the more successful your organization will be. One of the best tools to bring alignment is a strong organizational culture. One of the best ways to develop strong organizational culture are strong, numerous, and diverse teams.

One Example – SLTs

Strategic Leadership Teams (SLTs) are teams within an organization which work in some way for the future success of the organization. While every organization has teams of some sort, SLTs put the emphasis more on *strategic* goals for the organization. These goals could be varied but one unique aspect of the SLT is its influence. The SLT is supposed to, "send consistent signals throughout the organization," and to influence each other on the team as well as influence the rest of the organization" (Hughes, R. L. & Beatty, K. C., 2005, 183-186). As we develop strategic teams, they become a good example of how we can use teams to creatively establish a strong organizational culture because these teams have the highest probability of impacting the entire organization.

In forming strategic teams, Bradford & Duncan (2000) state that strategic teams should have a, "variety of personalities, backgrounds, and thinking styles – and people who will express their thoughts" (p. 13). While we want a variety of backgrounds, we also want people who have, "direct influence on the course of the company and day-to-day responsibility" (p. 15). In the example of SLTs, we try to pull together not only talented people, but also different people. These different people bring their own individual expertise, but also different realms of influence throughout the organization. This could be different segments of the organization, such as people from finance, marketing, and operations, or also from different circles of influence through natural relationships within the organization.

I'd like us to think a little further than the possible reaches of an SLT. Could we call it a KB Leadership Team? While SLTs are vital to an organization, there are creative ways to pull in the "extended family" of your company to help create the culture you desire. Imagine a new secretary or data entry specialist who has been with your company less than a month. While they may not be chosen for an SLT, they could still be a part of impacting your organization's culture and could provide invaluable assistance. In the same way a long time associate has expertise that could make them a top choice for an SLT, a new person's "new" or outside perspective could provide expertise to impact the organization's culture. By reaching out to people at all levels in your organization, you are enforcing a culture that values people and lets your employees know that they matter. If you take their input seriously and even make changes based on their input, one natural side product will be visible signs that you as a leader value your staff and you will see an increased employee loyalty.

Now if you are a leader in your organization I don't want to burst your bubble, but while you may be in one of the best positions to influence others, there are many others who can and will influence your organization. In a very simple sense – people influence people.

There are countless stories in leadership books where the CEO bumps into a janitor or cafeteria worker and begins to ask how their experience has been at the company. Often times their input is very helpful to the CEO and the employee feels a new sense of loyalty and excitement for being a part of a company where the CEO cares and listens. This is what millions of people watch on TV on the show, *Undercover Boss*. This is a part of using an organization wide approach in forming your organization as a team, or family, or a place where people know they are valued and are listened to. We all want to be part of a place where everyone knows our name, don't we? We all want to be valued, we all want to contribute, and simply put we all want to matter.

SLTs help us see that teams should not be just about accomplishing a task, but also about influence. Leaders can and should use teams to influence and help create desired culture in their company. In many ways how this is done depends upon the size of the organization, but the point is that the more you move away from being a single fighter and relying on your organization as your team, the closer you are to holding the key to unlock the potential of an organization with a powerful culture.

Size Matters

"I often look at organizational teams as track teams or basketball teams." This is what a friend once told me. He felt that most organizations functioned more like a track team; one large team, but everyone having their own specialty. Is your organization a larger team comprised of many smaller "specialists" just like a track team with your sprinters, distance runners, jumpers, shot putters, etc.? Or are you like a basketball team? A smaller team working closely together, essentially all trying to accomplish one goal, while having slightly different positions within your team? At the time I was leading a "basketball team." No, not really a sports team, but a branch office with a small staff. We were all very close, and while we all had different roles and different strengths, we all took part in the planning together and most of the activities together. The staff would often comment about how closely we worked together using words like family, unity, solid, fun, strength and one purpose.

If you are leading a team or an organization which is smaller, it will naturally be easier to influence and change culture. The larger your organization is, the longer, harder, and slower changing your organization's culture will be. While the challenge may be greater to influence organizational culture in a larger organization, people are still your greatest asset. While your organization may always function like a track team, the more you help your organization to feel like a "team," the more you will be able to impact your culture. Once you establish an appealing culture (or work environment), people from other organizations may even desire to come and work with you simply because of the culture and climate for which your company is known. People want to be a part of something bigger than themselves and be in a place they enjoy doing it. This is what happened at our branch center. Once we had worked towards establishing a strong team culture we had people from similar branches in other cities desire to come and join us.

The more people who are onboard with you as the leader, the vision, and the way things are done, the easier it is to modify and tweak aspects of culture. This in and of itself is a part of culture, and usually a difficult one to accomplish. Let's call it adaptability and flexibility. Don't forget the value and necessity of a team in creating culture in your organization. I hope you're encouraged not to be a lone ranger.

Even though the show was before my time, I remember seeing occasional re-runs of *The Lone Ranger*. I thought it was interesting that even the "Lone" Ranger was really not alone; he always had Tanto, didn't he? Every great coach has a great team. Every successful quarterback has a solid offensive line, running backs, tight ends, and wide receivers. No company becomes great simply because of a great leader. Even Jesus had the disciples. Developing a "team" culture is not only about succeeding in your business, but about legacy. You are investing in the lives of people. What you sow in these lives has the potential to carry on from generation to generation.

Leadership was never meant to be an isolated series of events. Senge (2006) says that successful learning organizations are organizations by the people, for the people. The creation and influencing of organizational culture can never succeed unless we understand the necessity of a team in helping to build a dynamic organizational culture.

Discussion Questions

1. Who would you say is "on" your team? What are their roles?

2. Have you ever (or do you know others who have) functioned as a single fighter? What were the strengths? What were the weaknesses? How could having a team have helped overcome the weaknesses?

3. Do you have a team you would consider an "SLT"? Who is on it? Describe your thought process in why you selected these people? Have the results been what you desired? Why or why not?

4. If you don't have an "SLT" - why not? Who would you select to be a part of a SLT and why? How would their ability to influence others impact your decision?

5. Ask five trusted people in your organization which employees they think should be on some type of leadership team and aren't. What did they tell you? Do you know these people? Why didn't you choose them?

6. Make a point of meeting with some of your newest employees (make sure they're from different departments if you can) who have been there less than six months. Ask them questions to help you learn about their feelings, ideas, and input for you (the leader), their superiors, and how the organization could improve. What did you learn?

7. When I say, "Let's meet for coffee," what place comes to mind? If you're like most Americans you'd answer Starbucks. Interestingly enough a study of the CEO, founder, and leader of Starbucks, Howard Schultz, is an eye opening study of leadership styles. He actually left leadership for a number of years and then recently returned as CEO. Since his return, Starbucks has been on the rebound and improving. I recently read an article that said he's just as

passionate, but a very different man; humble, more open minded, listens to others, asks questions, and is more of a team player. I'm sure this is one of the key reasons for Starbucks' recent improvement.

8. If you are in a position of leadership, list 5-10 things you could do better in terms of working with others, and leading as a team. Better yet, ask some people from different levels of seniority in each of your departments to tell you. Use the blank space below to write out your list(s).

Chapter 7

Corporate Warming or "Are You in the Ice Age"?

Organizational Climate is One of the Best Gauges of Organizational Culture

Most of us know that places like Indonesia are hot. There's just no escaping it. I walk to the kitchen to get a drink and I can already feel the sweat building on my brow. I've given up to the fact that I'll always feel hot in Indonesia. In 10 years here, I've only worn a jacket about half a dozen times and those were to protect myself from the sun, not because I was cold. We don't even have defrosters in our cars here in Indonesia because there's only a need for ACs. But I've also been extremely cold here; colder than I usually have ever felt in the US, more specifically in my home area of Northern California. Those of us who ride motorcycles know that riding a motorcycle on a windy, rainy day with no jacket can be downright freezing.

Many weather images can help us understand the concept of organizational climate. Organizational climate is not your culture, but it is one of the clearest gauges of your organizational culture. The easiest way to understand organizational climate is what an organization *feels like* when you walk through the doors and spend time inside either following the policies, interacting with the people, looking around, trying to get assistance, or trying to get your work done. In the same way we immediately feel the climate outside of our houses we can quickly "feel" what an organization is like.

I remember one summer in high school when we were having a very hot week in my home town. The daily high temperatures were all above 100 degrees, at times up to 115 degrees. Thank God there was hardly any humidity; it was a "dry heat." I had gone to see a movie with some friends early in the afternoon. We enjoyed the cool, air-conditioned theater and our ice-cold drinks. The movie finished and we walked outside. The air was so hot, so dry, that I felt like I lost my breath for a second. As I stepped out onto the asphalt, I literally felt waves of heat hitting my body. All I wanted to do was to go back into the theater. There was no way to escape the heat, no matter what I did unless I went back into the theater. The climate in our organizations will be different and may differ from day to day, week to week, but there should be a general feel in our offices and teams that people are unable to escape – that's our typical organizational climate.

What's Your Climate Like?

Certain theories about culture state that an organization creates its own culture. This culture represents what the organization stands for. In the end the culture itself becomes a powerful tool of communication; specifically communication of values and priorities which we know directly impact organizational culture. We therefore, create a worldview within our organizations which exhibit a reality. The organizational culture theory states that, "In talking about culture we are really talking about a process of reality construction that allows people to see and understand particular events, actions, objects, or situations in distinctive ways" (Littlejohn & Foss, 2008, p. 269). As we have already seen, these things in turn influence our company's choices and actions.

As we think more of our company's culture, we must realize that a culture will create an internal climate which will impact all daily activities and interactions. Poole and McPhee note that, "climate is a collective attitude, continually produced and reproduced by members,' and the general collective description of the organization that shapes members' expectation and feelings and therefore the organization's performance" (Littlejohn & Foss, 2008, p. 263). So the climate is not something that is pre-existing, but something which leaders and followers create based upon their interactions, choice and values. Whatever values we hold to create a culture within our organizations, and the way we live these out daily, will create a unique and specific organizational climate. Some climates encourage growth and communication while others make it difficult to achieve our goals.

The key question is, "What is our organization's climate? What do people sense when they walk through our doors? Is this the climate that we want?" Our current organizational climate gives excellent clues to the type of organizational culture we currently have.

Remember: The Two Can't Be Separated

Culture and climate are inseparable, but also different things. Shockley-Zalabak states that, "the reaction to an organization's culture is the organization's communication climate" (p. 48). What we communicate and how we communicate shows what our culture is. We see this in Indonesia often. There are over 300 different ethnic groups with the Javanese, Sundanese and Madurese being some of the larger ethnic groups, but the Javanese are the largest and most dominant. They are not dominant in terms of having a domineering personality, but in terms of being the more "desirable" or "preferred" group. Practically every Indonesian president has been Javanese. One of the negative aspects of so many cultures is that racism is very common. We've seen Javanese people often talk down to other "less desirable" ethnic groups. The accepted culture or norms here impacts the ethnic climate as seen in communication between ethnic groups.

Cameron & Quinn make a great comparison between culture and climate stating,

> "Climate refers to more temporary attitudes, feelings, and perceptions on the part of individuals. Culture is an enduring, slow-changing core attribute of organizations; climate, because it is based on attitudes, can change quickly and dramatically. Culture refers to implicit, often indiscernible aspects of organizations. Culture includes core values and consensual interpretations about how things are; climate includes individualistic perspectives that are modified frequently as situations change and new information is encountered" (Cameron, K. S. & Quinn, R. E., 2006, p. 147).

While culture is the more long-lasting element, it is also more difficult to change. Climate can change quickly just like a storm which suddenly blows in from off shore, but what often blows in the storm (or calms the water). is our organization's culture.

Because of this, keep in mind that our organization's climate is not static, but active. Just like the weather can change from day to day, our climate may change. This may make you question the strength of using organizational climate as a gauge of culture. While both culture and climate are influenced by people, the climate is more prone to be impacted by people's moods and experiences. Littlejohn & Foss (2008) remind us that climate is constantly in the process of development. Try to think of what your climate is on a "typical" day. While no day may be the same as the next, in general, our organizations do have a "typical" day. This could be related to many "typical" things such as the typical attire, typical interactions between people, typical conversations, typical ways to answer phones, typical ways to receive guests, typical decorations in your office, and even typical meetings or the typical lunch hour. If your organization is larger, you could even experience different climates in different groups within your organization. How a group does things is because of their culture and this creates a climate which is felt by others. Schein (2009) states that organizational climate is, "the feeling that is conveyed in a group by the physical layout and the way in which members of the organization interact with each other, with customers, or with other outsiders" (p. 15).

These "typicals" will portray a climate which is not only conveyed by your staff, but also felt by everyone internally and externally, but outsiders or new staff may be your best asset in understanding your organization's current climate.

You Need Outsiders

Who are probably some of the worst people to gauge your organizational climate?

Leaders and long-term, highly committed staff.

Have you ever not seen a friend for a long time and when you finally see them they comment on how much you changed? It may be (hopefully) that you look so much skinnier, healthier, or happier, but as they make a comment like that you find yourself asking, "Am I really skinnier?" You go home and ask your spouse, "Honey, do I look skinnier to you?" "I guess," is the response, followed by, "but I think you look about the same." It's the same if you have children. When you haven't visited a friend or extended family member for a long time and then you finally see each other, they often can't get over how BIG your kids have gotten. While you've noticed they've definitely grown, they haven't grown THAT much, have they? The problem in both situations is that when you see something every single day, it's difficult to sense any change; it's simply the norm, or your reality.

This is similar to the example used about placing a frog in boiling water. If you haven't heard the example that is often quoted about change, the basic story is that if you place a frog in boiling water, they will get out as fast as they can, but if you place a frog in water, slowly heat up the water and bring it to a boil they will stay in and eventually die. Why? They didn't notice the change, and missing the changes that were going on around them eventually lead to their death. Our organizational climate is the same.

If you've been in your organization long enough you may not even be aware of your climate, or may have difficulty explaining it accurately. You need people who are not used to your culture and climate to help you see what your climate is. If you're outside on a hot day and the temperature increases ten degrees you may not even notice it, but if you're inside a cool, air-conditioned room, you notice the heat the second you walk outside your front door. Outsiders can help you know your climate. They can be the best way to gauge your climate through what they see and feel from your organization and your employees.

People may have difficulty explaining deeper aspects of culture, but in terms of the climate, outsiders can easily describe what they see and feel. Whether through formal and informal surveys, comment cards, strategic conversations, or phone interviews, anyone considered an outsider (whether that be a new staff member, customer or stranger) offers the best perspective on your climate. Remember while your climate is always developing, it's a great tool to help you gauge where your culture is at.

Which Came First?

Performance and climate are often linked together. Does success create a positive or desired climate, or does the actual climate bring about increased performance and success? Hughes & Beatty (2005) state that there is a complex interaction between performance and climate (p. 77-79). We could essentially change "performance" with many other words that we desire for our organizations, but to make it easier, let's consider performance similar to success; it's anything we desire to achieve in our organizations. It is the sign that we are performing as desired and on track to accomplish our goals and achieve our dreams. So which came first, performance or climate?

I remember singing a song that was on Sesame Street, "which came first, the chicken or the egg?" In the same way, which came first, performance or climate? Does our strong and positive climate lead to our success or does our success lead to an appealing climate? I like to think that the answer to that question is "Yes" to both. As Hughes & Beatty note, performance and climate are so deeply intertwined that it isn't something which can be neatly separated and analyzed. Aziza & Fitts (2008) link this climate of performance to culture stating that, "organizations achieve a competitive advantage when they develop a culture that fosters improved performance" (p. 19). They go on to state that this performance is highly connected to the organization's credibility. An organization desiring more credibility needs to also increase a climate and culture of performance. Performance and climate are more of a reinforcing loop where both actions influence more of the same action resulting in growth.

Six years ago I went to a meeting in Atlanta. The meeting was at a public relations and marketing office which worked with groups in promoting events, book releases, or promoting actual organizations. I was there to sit in on a meeting about promoting an upcoming book. From the moment I walked in, I was impressed. Everyone was very professional, and very warm. The office was very well laid out and showed pictures of well known figures and events they had helped succeed. As we sat down in the meeting with about six of their lead staff, they all started by stating which sections of the book they liked the best, what it communicated to them, and what they felt were good approaches to promoting the book. I was highly impressed, no actually a bit in shock. They all came across as successful people and were ready to give everything they had to help this book succeed. They had done their homework, given thorough thought to marketing strategies, met with one another prior to our meeting and prepared a very impressive presentation. They also were open to dialogue and wanted to listen as well. The climate was very impressive, and it felt like things would be very successful; or was it that it was so successful that it made things feel impressive? Actually, it was both.

If you want a climate which breeds performance and want to increase your performance to develop your desired climate, you need to think of it as a reinforcing loop that can't be separated. Having the right culture becomes the foundation for creating a positive reinforcing loop, and isn't that what we're working for?

Desired Climate Isn't Too Hard to Define

What do you set your thermostat at? Maybe some of us set it at 78 degrees, others 75, while come like it cooler at about 70 degrees, but we all have a climate that we like. It's pleasant, comfortable, and enjoyable and doesn't hinder anything we're doing. The more we're used to it, the more we might not even notice the actual climate. Have you ever stepped into water that felt "just right"?

Living in Indonesia, I'm usually hot. If it's too hot of a day I get sunburned pretty bad riding my motorcycle around, but also since we're close to the equator we have a pretty wet rainy season. Certain days I plan to go out, I may be forced to stay in, because it's pouring down rain and the streets are flooded. My ideal climate is very similar to what people prefer here; fairly clear, a slight breeze, warm, but not hot, and dry (no rain!). But when I ask people in Indonesia what the favorite season is (hot season or rainy season) almost every Indonesian will answer rainy season because during hot season the sun is out all day and it is hot, so hot that you get a nice tan, which the typical Indonesian doesn't want (they like lighter skin). If I were to answer the same question, I would never answer rainy season because the rain seems to hinder so many things causing flooded streets, leaky roofs, and more frequent power outages. Besides, during hot season I get a nice tan, which I like.

In the same way we all have preferences to a certain climate (or weather), we all have fairly specific desires when it comes to the climate of our organizations and offices. Think of organizations which you like. How would you describe them? Think of your ideal office setting. What does it feel like? Maybe your list would include things like a place that is positive, encouraging, challenging, the people respect each other, innovative, supportive, fun, refreshing and honest. I think it's a fairly safe bet that our lists of things we would want to feel when we walk through the door of our ideal organization probably wouldn't differ very much. Most people want some sort of "positive" climate.

Most successful organizations also foster a climate of learning. Simply think of a team which is led by someone who is a good leader verses someone who is not. Which would you prefer? I love it when leaders who have so much more training, so much more experience, and such better results than me actually sit down with a pen and paper and begin to ask me for my opinion on something. It's amazing! I don't only feel valued, but valuable; I feel that I have something to offer and that I matter.

When I first came to Indonesia I was young. In Indonesian standards I'm still young (which I don't actually mind now), but it made it very difficult to work with some leaders. One group I worked with was led by an older man. Let's just say that the climate in his organization was very formal. I found out quickly that he never asked for any input from me, let alone his other staff. Once I had spoken to a large group and he closed the meeting by publicly rejecting the ideas I had just proposed. After months working with this man I was sharing with him my father-in-law's story, who is now a well-known speaker and author. It just so happened that this Indonesian man aspired to be a well-known speaker, teacher and author. In that story I shared some things that my father-in-law had done in his organization. To my surprise the Indonesian man did the same things the next week. After that, I knew how to communicate my ideas to the leader – say my father-in-law did it. But of course, I would only say that if I knew that my father-in-law would agree to it. We all want to be valued. Being around leaders who are learners helps create a climate which values people – and we not only like that; we need that.

Having a climate of learning also leads to a more strategic culture. Hughes and Beatty (2005) explain how fostering a climate of learning doesn't only help teams to act strategically, but that it also develops strategic action in others (p. 181). Daft (2008) states that, "culture plays an important role in creating an organizational climate that enables learning and innovative response to challenges, competitive threats, or new opportunities" (p. 429). Begin now to imagine how not only the right culture, but the right climate can help your organization to be strategic about future growth.

Ask outsiders how they feel about your organization, products and staff. Listen to them. This climate is an expression or reflection of your culture. What do people feel as they walk through your doors? Is the weather nice or do they feel like they just entered the ice age? Do they like what it feels like in your organization or do they quickly want to leave? Understanding your climate can help you understand and change your culture. Having the right culture and climate may be one of the best tools to help you respond quicker and more accurately to external forces your organization will encounter. In a sense they may both be some of the best tools to not only ensure your future survival, but your future success.

Discussion Questions

1. Keeping in mind images of weather, how would you describe the climate of your organization and why?

2. What adjectives would you want someone new, who just walked through your doors, to use in describing your organization?

3. Talk about the last storm (or problem/challenge) that blew through your organization. How did your people respond to it? How did it impact the "feel" in your organization? What does this show you about the culture and climate of your organization?

4. If you had to choose one word (and one word only) to describe what people feel when they walk through your doors, what word would you choose? Why?

5. What are some things customers have told you about your organization or staff that have been most helpful to bring change? What have they told you in the past that you ignored but actually need to pay attention to?

6. What are some tools you could create to learn from customers and better understand your organizational climate? What tools do you

already have (formal/informal surveys, comment cards, online forms, phone interviews, etc.)?

7. Describe the climate on a "typical" day at your organization.

8. How would you describe your ideal office climate? Now ask five other people to describe their ideal office climate? What words were used?

Chapter 8

Outside-In Not Wrong Side-Out

Organizational Culture's Response to External Change

While we all know this, we have to remember that we are never working in isolation. There are internal and external forces, shifts, and trends which will constantly impact us. Most often organizations end up being reactionary, simply reacting to forces which they encounter, dealing with them, and continuing on. Thankfully with all of the development in strategic foresight in the past couple of decades, organizations are beginning to see the value of trying to understand the times so that they can be more robust in encountering the future. We will talk more specifically about strategic shifts in the next chapter, but one of the more strategic shifts you can make is to build a culture which is proactive, not reactive, and can respond appropriately, quickly and efficiently to external change which you will face. Organizations with iron walls living in isolation rarely, if ever, end up protecting themselves as they hoped. The question isn't *if* you'll face some unexpected external change, but *when*?

When I was living in Fiji I took a journey to some outer islands. While Fiji is a country of islands, the two main islands, Viti Levu and Vanua Levu account for about 75% of the nation's land area and most of the population lives there. I was living on the main island, Viti Levu, and we set out on a medium-sized boat in the middle of the night to my friend's island. We rocked back and forth for 15 hours before we finally arrived. It was a small island, although large enough to live on and looked safe enough for the village there. There was only one village on the entire island which had about 150 people living there. We stayed for one week. I was amazed how isolated it was. When it came time for me to head back, I asked some of the villagers if we were going back to the main island the next day as planned. "Go to the capitol! No, not for another one to two weeks, we don't have enough fish to sell yet," was their response. "*WHAT!*" was what I thought, but thankfully I didn't answer that way. I explained to my friend that I had commitments on the main island which couldn't wait. He understood. They called the leaders of the village together and they came up with a plan to get me back.

On a neighboring island there was a village where a cruise ship always stopped and brought their guests ashore. They came ashore for an evening meal in a "traditional" village to see traditional dancing, and a chance to buy handicrafts. I was to go to this island and catch a ride back to the capital on the cruise ship. It sounded like a great idea to me; relaxing in a lounge chair for a few hours on my way back to the capitol, and I'd never been on a cruise ship. We were ready for the festivities to begin, the band and some important area leaders had come out by helicopter, and the villagers had everything ready. We saw the ship coming, it neared the dock which had been constructed a ways out from the island. The smaller boats were there to shuttle people to the beach. The ship neared the dock, and kept on going. *What!*? I thought again, although this time it was harder to hold it in.

Because there was a storm coming, the ship decided not to stop so they could avoid rough seas and get to port in the capitol before the storm. I asked my friend how I was supposed to get back now. He went to see what he could do, and 20 minutes later he came back and said, "Steve, you're going to go back in the helicopter." "*WHAT!*" I exclaimed (but this time in excitement). I've always wanted to ride in a helicopter. So I sat back on the beach and waited to go. I noticed they were getting the helicopter ready, people were boarding, and it looked like it would leave soon. I asked my friend when I should go and at that exact moment the helicopter lifted off and left. "*WHAT!*" Which as you could image by now had become my theme word for the day. We began to look for different options and there was only one left – a big enough, although top- heavy boat which was going back to the capitol.

While I did get on this boat, the ride was one of the worst I've ever had on a boat. Since the boat was built a little too high for its length, we were bobbing back and forth for seven-eight hours. Out of 50 people on board, at least 35 got sick. We finally made it back and when we walked through the door of our hotel, our friends embraced us with tears. "What's wrong?" I asked. What we didn't know is that a number of ships had capsized in the area because of the storm and a number of lives were lost. Our friends thought our boat may have been one of them since we were in the same area.

Living in isolation limits our options, but it does not mean that you can't be adaptable, flexible, and able to respond quickly to external changes. Having a culture which can anticipate and respond quickly to external forces and change increases your options and possibilities of success as you embrace the future.

Stuff Happens

Let's face it – the world is going to go forward whether we're ready for it or not. Change will come whether we like it or not. Some competitors will fade away while new competition will rise up. Consumers will change their tastes, patterns and styles. Throughout all of this we're trying to not only keep up, but to stay ahead. But is it really possible?

I think it is.

While we can't anticipate everything and can be caught off guard, there are more and more tools to help us function in a proactive way, opposed to a reactive way. The biggest issue in this chapter is uncertainty. Our futures are uncertain, but the more certainty we can have, the more informed our choices, the more appropriate our strategy, and the more successful we can become.

I remember watching a television show where a man was transported to the future. When he came back to the present time he already knew which sports teams would win. He bet on all the right teams and made a ton of money. We know this doesn't happen. While we can plan and prepare for the future, we are not in control of it. Many of us don't even know what's just around the corner. We know that a major issue in achieving our dreams is dealing with uncertainty. How can we create a culture which can respond appropriately to future uncertainties? Can we use organizational culture as a strategic tool to respond better to the future?

I think so.

From Layers to Levels

We talked earlier in chapter two about the layers (or webs) of culture. Thompson (1967) lines up a model of levels when dealing with decision making in light of future uncertainty. Thompson's work was related to the nature of uncertainty and how it impacts or determines the needed structure of our organization. There are variables in our market or environment which cannot be predicted. While we seek to understand the external environment as much as possible, we also need to understand ourselves and our own organization. We need to create, or structure our organization to be able to thrive in our current environment, especially in terms of being prepared to face uncertainty. At the same time our organizations must "shield" or protect our core from uncertainty. One example from organizational culture is our key values. We must protect those and hold on to those so that future uncertainty does not cause our foundations to be shaken. External forces, trends and change cannot always be predicted and even less often can be guided or manipulated. We can set up components within our organization to interact with external change while at the same time internally protecting our core. We can create our core to help us achieve maximum performance while at the same time creating other aspects within our structure to be uniquely prepared to engage with external forces and uncertainty. There are levels that get closer or farther from our "core". Thompson's third level, the institutional level, covers aspects within our organization which deal with higher levels of uncertainty and where we may encounter less control. Thompson feels that technology and our environment need to impact how we structure our organization. The size, focus, and your leadership style will also come into play in organizational structure, but all of these forces should be taken into account as we create organizational culture which can thrive in the face of uncertainty.

Do You Use a Compass or a Map?

Hopefully both.

Driskill & Brenton (2011) give a helpful illustration of organizational leaders using a compass or a map. When we are creating strategy and making decisions, too often we act more as if we are using a map. We need to take road A to this city, then go east on road B to the following city, we follow that to the east for six hours and when we intersect with road C, we turn south for so many miles, and so on. But life doesn't happen like that, does it? While we can drive places like that, we can't necessarily live life and lead our organizations like that. Uncertainty causes us to need to engage the future with compasses. Driskill & Brenton (2011) state that, "there is value in using a compass rather than a map; both are good, but a compass allows you to say, 'I don't know exactly where I'm going but I know I'm not lost'" (p. 115-116). With a compass we still have a sense of direction, a sense of where we are now, and know we're on the right track, but we also aren't predicting what we could encounter in the future which could potentially throw us off our current path.

Think with me for a second. If you walk through a heavily forested area with no paths, you're trailblazing. You can't always walk in straight lines. If you did so, you'd probably hit a number of trees; but you can weave your way through obstacles and still head in the right direction and reach your final destination.

This is similar to the concept of commander's intent that we talked about earlier. If your team knows where you are going and the end goal, you can allow for mid-course adjustments without losing sight of the end goal. You can create your organization to be one where your core values or inner level as Thompson (1967) talks about, can be protected, but your other levels can help you lead to affectively weave through unexpected obstacles and still stay on track with your overall strategic plan.

We need a map to give us direction and help us choose destinations, but during the journey it may be more helpful to rely on a compass which assures us that we're still on track even if life causes us to take alternative routes.

It's Like a *"Jalan Tikus"*

What's your image of a rat? It's negative isn't it? Possibly words that come to your mind are "dirty" or "a pest." In the US if we call someone a rat, it's definitely not positive. In Indonesia the definition is a little different. Rats are still dirty and people don't really like them, but Indonesians give rats a little credit. If you ask an Indonesian to describe a rat they'll most likely say, *"cerdik"* which means clever.

This comes mainly from the fact that rats can get in and out of almost anything, anywhere, any time. House construction is different in Indonesia than in the US. We have rats regularly in our roof, finding ways into rooms, in the drainage pipes, running across telephone wires, along our fence tops, and of course, they nightly scurry all over our backyard lawn. No matter how hard I've worked to close off our roof, it seems that rats can still easily find holes to get in and run across our ceilng, store their food, or even nest. If a route is shut down, they don't stop. They simply look for a different route and eventually get into wherever they want.

Here the term, "*jalan tikus*" (*jalan* = street or path and *tikus* = rat) was invented. It basically means alternative route in terms of using public roads. If you use back streets, short cuts and small streets, you know many *jalan tikus*. This is especially helpful in times of traffic jams (a daily occurrence in Indonesia), flooding or streets that are closed for construction or community ceremonies. Indonesians are very impressed when foreigners have mastered the art of taking a *jalan tikus*.

While we hopefully spend a lot of time and resources in planning strategically for our future, even our best efforts do not guarantee that we will always be right about the future. In some markets there are high levels of uncertainty. In these markets the external trends and forces cycle more and we must be ready to respond quicker to external change.

Daft (2008) states that, "if the competitive environment requires speed and flexibility, for example the culture should embody values that support adaptability, collaboration across departments, and a fast response to customer needs or environmental changes" (p. 425). To be successful in encountering the future we really need to understand our environment and also who we are as an organization. One of the greatest forces we can control is the internal culture in our organization that we create, support and sustain. One term that has surfaced in terms of organizational culture is that of a "strong" culture, but a strong culture is not enough; we also need an efficient and adaptable culture. This is one which culturology presumes; a culture where an organization knows their core, but also is adaptable in terms of dealing with external forces and change and efficient in dealing with these forces. Daft (2008) states that while many organizations develop strong cultures which encourage teamwork, collaboration and mutual trust, this is not enough. In adaptive cultures leaders are also concerned about people being able to respond to change. Leaders who create strong, adaptive, and efficient cultures in their companies care deeply about customers and employees; they seek to serve the entire organization. An organizational culture like this helps us to protect the core and engage the fringe; helps us to follow our map while using a compass, and helps us to reach our destination while relying on a "*jalan tikus*" whenever needed.

Using Uncertainty to Your Advantage

Could we actually take advantage of uncertainty? Some feel it can become a strategic tool for us to use with our organizations in creating our ideal organizational culture.

It is a bit of reverse psychology, but some people feel that we can create and use uncertainty to develop cultural traits which we desire, namely quicker responses to uncertainty and a higher level of cooperation between different people or departments within our organization. Michel and Wortham (2009) compare two banks and how they dealt with uncertainty and chaos. In their study they found that the chaos caused more chaos for the banks examined, but also strengthened them. They state that as leaders, managers, and other employees encountered something they didn't have the tools to deal with, they were forced to collaborate together and by doing this their organization became stronger (p. 220-221). Because of this, they feel that uncertainty amplification may be a viable strategy for organizations to be more prepared in dealing with the unexpected.

We do not live in a vacuum. One way to make sure that we are more prepared for uncertainty is to look for controlled ways we can actually create chaos. Another approach would be to simply be intentional about dealing with the unknowns of the future that are out of our control. The organization which increases their ability to respond appropriately to uncertainty will be strategically positioned to succeed. Aziza & Fitts (2008) also link this to the ability of an organization to analyze the future effectively. They state that, "being deficient in the monitoring capability can result in: shortsightedness, managing by conjecture and sounds bites, aimlessness and speculation, misalignment, and inability to execute strategy. And this in turn leads to missed opportunities and uninformed planning" (p. 40-43).

The goal is not necessarily to hire more analysts, but to help everyone who is currently part of your team to view themselves as an analyst who helps monitor the horizon for your organization. This could be through interactions with customers, investors, surfing the web, seeing what comes up through their social networks, other companies from similar markets, staying in tune with competitors, and increasing communication and trust within your organization. The better we are able to analyze and understand a situation, the better we can deal with uncertainty. Aziza & Fitts (2008) suggest that we need to empower our staff analysts to decide what's important to measure. Once there is greater communication and trust, we will begin to see a culture which is able to thrive in light of uncertainties and this is needed if we are going to gain a competitive edge in our markets in today's rapidly changing world.

It's not enough to simply be able to analyze and monitor the horizon, but to be able to interpret and understand what we see. Since the tsunami that rocked Indonesia and surrounding nations in 2004, we've become more aware of tsunamis, especially with the most recent and destructive tsunami in Japan in 2011. While over 200,000 died from the Indonesia tsunami of 2004, a small island, very close to the epicenter, suffered very few casualties. Out of the 75,000 inhabitants, only seven people died. How can this be? They know not only how to scan the horizon, but how to understand it. People from the island of Simeulue in Indonesia have stories passed down from their ancestors about the last time a tsunami hit their island. A villager was quoted saying, "If I feel an earthquake I look for the water (ocean) to suck out. If the water sucks out, I run to the hills." People waited in the hills for over an hour because of seeing the ocean suck out or recede. By the time the tsunami hit their island, practically everyone was up on higher ground. In the Banda Aceh area, people also experienced the ocean receding, but most thought it was some blessing or freak of nature because as the ocean sucked out, countless numbers of fish were left on the sand bottom. People ran out onto the sand to collect the fish; it was going to be dinner for the next week, but sadly, three giant tsunami waves swept in and took all of their lives. It's not enough to simply monitor or scan the horizon, but we need to understand it so that we can respond quickly to changes around us.

We are not only shaping an organizational culture which is more primed to respond quickly and appropriately to external change, but we are helping to grow and develop our staff. Dealing with uncertainty can help your staff to increase their competence and skills set, possibly helping them develop new expertise in certain areas. After living in Indonesia for almost 10 years I have become an electrician, architect, construction worker, translator, negotiator, tour guide, roofer, painter, car and motorcycle mechanic and a doctor, just to name a few. Michel and Wortham (2009) remind us that we're not just building a business, but in the end we are leading people and in the end it is people who really matter the most. Making positive change and creating a strong and adaptable culture in your organization will help transform your staff into better, well rounded people. Ideally, as people encounter new ideas and concepts they will be open to different ways of learning. The actual job or job environment affects us all, but if we keep our staff in mind as we create and influence culture, we can also see people's lives transformed.

Uncertainty and Future Scenarios

Another tool that can be woven into the culture of your organization to help with uncertainty is scenario planning. Think of scenario planning as strategically thinking of all of the possible landscapes you may face. Some scenario planning may seem far-fetched (can we really know the future?), and some downright strange (when we think of extreme, highly unlikely scenarios), but in scenario planning we try to at least initially consider ALL of the possibilities so that we can think through how we could strategically plan if we had to take the road through the mountains or at the same time the road along the beach.

Ralston & Wilson (2006) state that, "uncertainty is more than incomplete and ambiguous information about individual forces and how they could play out in the future; it is the inspiration for the strategic thinking that occurs through the scenario-planning process" (p. 103). This process causes us to use the knowledge we have and consider the most likely futures. While we may not necessarily get it right, the future may very well be a combination of the potential landscapes we have already thought of. In this sense, building scenario planning into your organization's culture can also help you to deal with external change in your market.

Why take the time to create numerous future scenarios which may never be used? Ralston & Wilson (2006) feel that, "a primary objective of scenario planning is to reduce our vulnerability to surprises by forcing us to envision a variety of possible futures and to think through their implications for our organization" (p. 18). Scenario planning helps our staff to deal with external forces of change better and also to have stronger analytical skills as they monitor the horizon of our environment, market, and competitors.

One of the strengths of scenario planning is not just whether your team gets the actual future scenario "correct" or not, but that it begins to shape your organization's culture to be one where people are more future oriented and more prepared to deal with changes you will face. In many ways, it's just as much about the process as it is the end result. The process of scenario planning may dramatically reduce the impact of uncertainty on your organization both by having a strategy planned for potential scenarios, and by having employees who have been transformed by the potential future they are facing.

You Need to Close Your Eyes Once in a While

I learned something while working in a rehabilitation hospital in college – vision and points of reference are essential for balance and control. I thought of myself as a fairly athletic guy. I noticed that many patients were told to stand on large foam sponges and try to balance. Depending upon their injuries this was easy to impossible for them. Those who had been in rehab for a while and were getting more of their control back were then instructed to stand on the foam and close their eyes. Initially many almost fell over or at least took a large step and opened their eyes to catch themselves. Don't believe me? Why don't you stop reading this and try it for a second. Take your shoes off and stand on the floor, preferably in front of a mirror. Lift one leg off the ground and to the side of you. As you look at yourself in the mirror you may have to work at it, but most people can balance fairly well standing on one foot. Now standing in the same position close your eyes.

Did you have to work a lot harder to maintain your balance? Or were you even able to balance? Be honest, how many of you actually fell to one side and had to open your eyes? I know; me too.

Closing our eyes is similar to dealing with uncertainty and external change. The more reference points we have the more stable we will be to deal with changes; that's why having our eyes open and focusing on one thing helps us balance on one foot.

Cameron & Quinn (2006) state that, "Successful companies have developed something special that supersedes corporate strategy, market presence, and technological advantages. Although strategy, market presence, and technology are clearly important, highly successful firms have capitalized on the power that resides in developing and managing a unique corporate culture. This power abides in the ability of a strong, unique culture to reduce collective uncertainties" (p. 5).

If our responses to external change are informed and rapid, our company becomes more agile and able to respond quicker to external conditions. In the same way exercise increases your chance for a healthy future, developing a strong and adaptable culture which can respond appropriately to external changes can increase your chances of accomplishing your goals.

Change cannot be scheduled. There could be a gap between our planning and strategy and what we encounter. Having a culture that responds quickly to external change decreases this gap and helps maintain alignment. The degree to which a company can respond to outward forces and be adaptable allows them to be better prepared to handle an uncertain future. The main question isn't if you know the future, but are you preparing yourself, your staff and organization to be as ready as possible for any future that you'll face?

Discussion Questions

1. What are some major external forces or changes you've faced? How well (or poorly) did you respond to these?

2. Do you use a compass, a map, or both more often in your strategy and day to day operations? How could relying on a compass improve your organization and leadership?

3. Perform a SWOT analysis. List your greatest Strengths, Weaknesses, Opportunities, and Threats. Ask others in your organization to do this as well. How can you create a culture which can help you be more prepared to encounter the future and external forces? What are the major external forces you anticipate?

STRENGTHS:

WEAKNESSES:

OPPORTUNITIES:

THREATS:

4. How could the image of a "jalan tikus" help you in your leadership, training, and strategic planning?

5. Rate your organization's culture on a scale of 1-10 (10 being the highest)

    Strong -1 2 3 4 5 6 7 8 9 10

    Efficient -1 2 3 4 5 6 7 8 9 10

    Adaptable -1 2 3 4 5 6 7 8 9 10

Ask others in your organization to rate these three areas of your culture as well. What are some things you could do in each area to make your organization's culture stronger, more efficient, and more adaptable?

6. Do you use scenario planning? What have been the results? What are some ways you could implement a more proactive use of scenario planning?

7. List three possible scenarios of your organization's future?

8. Do you feel more prepared for any future you'll face, or do you expect you'll simply react to whatever comes your way? What are some shifts (in your culture) you could make so that your organization takes a more proactive stance towards external changes? Discuss this with your top leadership team. Use the rest of this page to list these needed shifts and important ideas from your discussion.

Chapter 9

Strategic Shifts

How to Use Organizational Culture as One of Your Primary Strategic Tools

In chapter three I shared about the "International" Suramadu 10-K race that our staff took part in. Everyone from our office took part in some way or another, but a majority of our staff decided to run the race. Different people on our staff approached the race differently. Two of us actually took it a bit seriously and started training for it, one did some training, two did no training, and the others decided to become the bag watchers and cheerleaders.

On the day of the race over 5,000 people showed up. The Kenyan team that I mentioned earlier was the automatic favorite. They were placed at the front of the start line, the gun sounded, and bang – they were off sprinting as fast as they could. I couldn't believe how fast they ran. From our staff's team I probably trained the hardest for the race. The Kenyan runners took all of the top positions, but I was happy that I actually beat two of them (but if I have to be honest I should tell you they both sprained their ankles mid-way and had to walk the rest of the race).

Even though I trained, there was no way that my training compared to the Kenyan's training. Even though I trained to try to compete I did not have the level of training needed to even hope to win. Now I'd like you to consider my two friends who did no training at all – what were their chances at competing with the Kenyans? Zero. Null. Nada. No way could they even dream of keeping up with the Kenyans.

In the same way we could never hope to win a race with no training, there's no way that we can achieve our goals if we do not develop a culture to support our strategic plans for the future. Putting an elaborate plan with BHAGs to motivate our staff to achieve great things, but not having a culture to support it is like jumping into a race against world class runners with absolutely no training and hoping that you'll beat them. While we take lots of time and spend lots of money on coming up with elaborate plans and goals, if we don't take the time to create the needed organizational culture to support the changes and actions of the future, it is like trying to build a house with no foundation. Our organizational culture is the foundation that helps become the bedrock to achieve greatness.

In the same way you shouldn't enter a running race without training, I hope you can see now that you shouldn't really jump to the future without creating a culture which will help support needed changes you desire to achieve.

Creating an organizational culture which will help you attain your goals may be one of the most important strategic steps in achieving your dreams. Aziza & Fitts (2008) state that, "a company's culture is a key factor in a company's strategy" (p. 209). Part of our strategy has to be to create the right organizational culture to allow for the growth we desire.

If a world class runner has trained appropriately, their mind is in the competition and they're much more ready to face whatever things they may encounter during their race. In the same way, having a strong, adaptable, and efficient organizational culture can help you to achieve your dreams while also being more prepared to face whatever things you may encounter along the way.

Strategic Steps for Culture Creation

How can we now begin to think strategically in making needed changes to our current organizational culture? Hughes & Beatty (2005) state that we should, "assess where you are, understand who you are and where you want to go, learn how to get there, make the journey, and check your progress" (p. 216). We all want to succeed. We also all want to enjoy the process – our day to day jobs and the dynamic of working together as a team. Using these steps to create our needed culture does not only strategically lay the ground work to help us succeed, but also creates an environment which we can enjoy and where people can be transformed.

Cameron & Quinn (2006) have a helpful process in moving from understanding our current culture to creating a new, needed culture.

1) Understand your current culture.

2) Reach consensus on the needed or desired future culture.

3) Look at which areas need to be emphasized more and less. What things need to be changed? And what will those changes mean?

4) Give good definitions and benchmarks. Identify illustrative stories.

5) Develop a strategic plan. Create activities which can be used to encourage the new/needed culture while also maintaining needed current aspects of your organization's

culture. It is very unlikely you need to scrap everything and start from scratch.

6) Make an action plan to implement helpful activities; some activities will be emphasized more and some will be deemphasized.

7) Evaluate and modify (p. 90).

Every organization has a certain culture. The biggest question we need to ask is if our current culture will enable us to achieve the future we desire. We need to think strategically not just about plans we'll make for the next month, quarter, year or five years, but we need to also think first if we have the needed organizational culture to support the future that we desire. In the same way running a race without training will never result in winning, making wonderful strategic plans without the needed organizational support will result in not reaching your full potential and your organization's desired future. Culturology is that something your organizational culture must pay attention to and use to your advantage.

Another Look at Strong, Strategic, and "Better" Cultures

Driskill & Brenton (2011) identify two cultures that are often considered "good." *Strong cultures* are good because their culture is very defined and clear. *Strategically appropriate cultures* are good because they support our defined or chosen strategy, but they identify a third culture which they call an "efficiently adaptive culture" which they state is better than a strong or strategically appropriate culture. This type of culture is able to flex and adapt better to whatever may come in the future. Driskill & Brenton refer to Collins (2001) stating that Collins, "based his theory of effective organizations on distinguishing companies that perform well in the short run verses those that have moved from "good to great" over a longer period of time. His analysis indicates that strategic fit is not the key to being a great organization" (p. 207). Having a culture which is efficiently adaptive is a culture which performs well over the long run. It is a culture which is strong in that it is well defined and is strategically appropriate in that it supports achieving your goals, but it is adaptive and can respond quickly to changes you will face in the future and can also do it in an efficient way.

A Surfing Culture?

I know what you're thinking? What does surfing have to do with business? Well, there are some very appropriate parallels between organizations and surfing.

I actually surf, not great, but I can ride waves. Some of my most enjoyable times are out in the ocean sitting on my surfboard with my friends taking turns trying to ride waves to the best of our ability, but at times the ocean is tough to read. Some sets of waves come in and are fairly small, but then suddenly a large set of waves will come through. If you're in the wrong position you'll get slammed, but if you can position yourself correctly, you can catch an incredible wave. The changes of the ocean and surfing don't stop there. Once you're on a wave you still need to adjust how and where you're riding, depending upon how the wave is breaking. Throughout the entire process there are constant changes all around you and you need to pay attention to everything that's happening around you. A surfer therefore is making constant decisions and changes based upon what is going on around them.

We had a friend who was called "wipe-out man." And if it's not obvious enough already, he got the nickname because he wiped out, a lot. His wipeouts were unique too. He didn't just fall off of his board, but he somehow would defy the laws of gravity and nature and come up with video worthy wipeouts. Our ability to read the waves, as well as react when we ride them, could cause us to rise to greatness or to experience some serious wipeouts in our organization.

A leader's role is much like a surfer navigating through the ocean, catching good waves, and making the most of each wave. Hughes & Beatty (2005) further related strategic leadership to surfing stating that, "strategic leadership is a bit like surfing. Both involve keeping your balance while learning the best path to follow amid constantly changing conditions. Your challenge now is to start moving on the path to more effective strategic leadership by developing your own and your team's thinking, acting, and influencing skills. This also happens to be your primary role in ensuring your organization's enduring success" (p. 228).

One crucial step in being strategic as a leader is developing an efficiently adaptive culture – this is a "surfing" culture. You've read many images throughout Culturology with the aim to show that cultures which are able to adapt to changes are the best cultures to achieve their dreams. One image was commander's intent, where the team knows the commanders intention or the overall goals and purpose of the operation, so that they can work with some freedom on the field as long as they keep their team on track in accomplishing the mission. Another image was how we should think more in terms of a compass and not a just a map in leading. A compass keeps us on track but also allows some freedom in slight changes or shifts along the way based upon what we face when we get to the future. Having a culture that is able to ride the waves of the future is one of the most strategic choices you can make. Taking the time to lay the right foundation and establish a culture like this in your organization not only increases involvement and creativity of your staff, but it increases your return on investment. If you invest in your organization in this way on the front end, the results will be felt in the future.

Hughes & Beatty (2005) state that there is no ONE best culture, but a culture that supports and doesn't constrain strategic leadership and strategy as a learning process is the ideal culture to help achieve goals (p. 201-204). Creating an efficiently adaptable culture will give your staff the skills needed to face the future. This will empower them to not be intimidated or overpowered by the waves they'll face, but to be able to creatively work together to overcome any challenges and respond to any threats while taking advantage of any opportunity so that your organization can ride the wave of the future to gain a competitive edge and see your own staff's lives develop in deeper ways.

Turn Up the Heat

Earlier we talked about organizational climate and the inseparable link between culture and climate, or what your organization "feels" like. In creating the right culture for your organization, you also will need to create the right climate. Your climate will impact all internal and external aspects of your organizations. The natural outcome of creating an advantageous culture for your organization will be that the climate within your organization will change as well.

One aspect of turning up the heat, or improving your organizational climate, is that there will be a feeling of increasing value. This is not just an improvement, but should be part of your strategy. If people, both internally and externally, value your organization more as well as feel valued, you will begin to see changes which will create momentum driving you closer to your goals. DeKluyver & Pearce (2009) also state that part of a good strategy is taking time to focus on creating value for shareholders, partners, suppliers, employees, and also the community (p. 7). Again, we see leaders pointing us to not only improve culture and climate to cause internal change, but that internal change should eventually translate into external impact as well. Certain aspects of your organization's culture may take more time to change, but as the change begins, you should begin to notice a shift in the climate fairly quickly. This of course will determine just how much change you feel you need, but the more change you make, the more noticeable the change in climate should be. It would be similar to walking from an air-conditioned room outside on a hot day; you notice the different climate right away. These changes are not simply about success, but also very much about the people we are working with, and even more so, about the world around us. One way we end up caring about the world is first caring about those we are leading.

Adamchik (2006) quotes John Woodmansee saying that, "the key to unleashing the potential of others in large part rests on creating the right climate in the organization. People who are uninspired by the nature of their work, lack confidence in their skills, are uncertain about their responsibilities, are concerned with being criticized for mistakes, and who rarely get feedback on performance, are unlikely to surprise you with high performance or innovation" (p. 113). While an entire book could also be written on organizational climate, in terms of culturology, my hope is that we can see how closely linked organizational culture and climate are and how strategic both are in achieving our dreams. You will begin to notice an immediate difference in climate as soon as steps to change needed aspects of our culture begin to occur. One of the reasons this is so essential is because it unlocks not only the potential within our organization, but the individual lives of our staff. As your staff begins to live inspired lives driven by passion to see change and to succeed, their passion will not only create an ever improving climate within your organization, but will also prepare you to take the next step in the change process. This change is one that I think often gets little attention since so many of us are worried about shareholders, market share, stock price and the bottom line.

I hope that through Culturology you can see that the final step in the change process lies beyond our doors, out in our communities, as well as around the world. It's something that's bigger than us with rewards that can't be measured in dollars and cents. It's called humanity. The world is waiting for people who will rise up and be ready to change the world.

Global Implications

I hope that by now we can agree that your influence can go far beyond yourself, even far beyond the walls of your organization. Turning into a culturologist and leading your organization to a healthier, stronger, more efficient, strategic, and adaptable culture is not designed to only help you gain a competitive advantage or increase your market share.

Do you believe in the power of one? I do.

Can one person really bring radical change to a community? To a city? To a nation? I'm too much of an optimist to answer, "No." But I know what you're thinking; there's no way it could be you, right? Wrong! The world is full of people, people who have incredible potential. People who have amazing gifts and wonderful talent, but you might feel that you're simply not one of "those" people. I think what the world needs isn't the most gifted, richest, smartest person, but someone who is simply willing. I wonder how different the world would be if we all intentionally took time to think through some ideas every week of what we could do to try to make the world a better place.

I was sitting in Starbucks last week when three ladies sat down at the table next to me. One advantage of being a foreigner (at times) in Indonesia is that strangers who sit down close to you assume you can't speak Indonesian so they talk freely about anything, feeling safe that you don't have a clue what's going on. It allows me some unique opportunities to learn how people talk among friends and even more interesting, what they talk about. One of these ladies was angry. She had purchased a purse and her husband was mad at her. She was upset because she felt she had been deceived. In her mind the purse was used, not new. She was angry that the person who sold it to her (which one of the other ladies had introduced her to) had tried to trick her by selling a used purse as new thus getting a lot more money. The third friend, neutral in all of this, kept saying things like, "hey, you saw it before you bought it...you should have checked it out...if you didn't like it you shouldn't have bought it." I was curious what the big deal was about the purse and why the husband was so upset until I heard the price – 50 million Rupiah (which is over $5,600.00)! I knew why the husband was upset. It wasn't because the bag was new or used, it was because the bag cost more than a decent used car! Now to put this in an Indonesian context, a common monthly salary is about 1 million Rupiah, or about $115 per month. What this woman had just spent on a purse was the equivalent of four years' salary for someone! While I'm no expert on purses, and it seemed like a nice-looking purse, I couldn't help but think how much of an impact that amount of money could have in a small poor Indonesian village, or giving a scholarship to a student for college (that would be enough for most 4-year colleges – ALL four years!). When we begin to think beyond ourselves and how our lives can begin to impact this world, we are beginning to think like a culturologist. Life is too short to simply live in our routines; get married, find a decent job, see our kids grow up, become empty nesters, retire, figure out where the time went, and finally look back and wish that we could have done more. The time has come to do more.

Driskill & Brenton (2011) state that, "organizations are realizing that environmental impact, community citizenship, financial stewardship, global development, and corporate responsibility are as important to evaluate as profitability in determining an organization's effectiveness" (p. 206). There's more to think about than just the bottom line. Often times we are so tunnel visioned by pressure from superiors or shareholders that we forget taking care of those around us also has value. A culture and climate that cares can also pay off in the end. Having the right set of values in our culture will create a trickle-down effect which will begin to impact much more than internal decisions. Driskill & Brenton (2011) also state that they find support for, "long-term, high-performing organizational cultures maintaining and passing on a value set focused on changing as needed" (p. 211). Once we have worked and created an organizational culture which is based on strong, clear values, have clear goals that we are seeking to accomplish, and have also created our culture to be adaptable to make needed changes based upon what we encounter in the future, a lot of things will simply take care of themselves.

You need to trust your staff. If we've taken into account issues raised in Culturology, and begin to address needed changes within our organizations and we've done this all alone or only with our lead team, then we've missed the point. Part of creating the needed culture to achieve your desired future is that you do it with others; at times including as many people as is logistically possible. One of your greatest resources is the people who are all around you.

Schein (2009) reminds us that, "Culture is a group phenomenon. It is a shared tactic of assumptions. Therefore, the best way to assess cultural elements is to bring groups together to talk about their organization in a structured way" (p. 220). We can't create culture without others and we can't maintain a desired organizational culture without others. And remember, the culture that we create can have implications far beyond our walls.

The world is in desperate need of people and organizations who will decide to do something beyond themselves. Schein (2009) goes on to state that we should, "Never start with the idea of changing a culture. Always start with the issues the organization faces, and only when those "business" issues are clear, ask yourself whether the culture will aid or hinder resolving the issues. Always think first of the culture as your source of strength" (p. 223). I'd like to add that once we get the "business" issues worked out, we still have a responsibility to those around us. Part of creating our needed organizational culture is not that we only take care of our business needs, but that in some way we can also begin to impact the world around us. Our culture should be a source of strength. Once it becomes one of our strengths, we can move beyond just business issues and move on to global issues.

Become a Culturologist

No one ever said that change was easy, and in recent years the word "change" has even gotten a negative connotation in certain circles, but I'm still a big fan of change – healthy change that will allow people to reach their maximum potential, your organization to achieve your desired future, and the world to be a better place, because people and organizations care enough to bring positive change to communities.

Cameron & Quinn (2006) remind us that changing culture is a, "difficult and long-term effort" (p. 101). While certain changes in our organizational culture can begin to change quickly, cultures are not something that are usually pliable enough to change rapidly, and actually changing rapidly could be counter-productive. While this change will take time, Schein (2009) also reminds us of the need for change stating that, "if you do not manage culture it will manage you and you may not even be aware of the extent to which this is happening" (p. 215).

We all need to improve our understanding of culture and the way our organizational culture can help or hinder us from attaining desired futures. Our staff, organizations, and even the world are waiting for culturologists to have eyes towards the future which are preparing people to efficiently adapt to changes that we will encounter tomorrow, next week, next year, and in the decades to come.

Some aspects of your organization's culture may amuse you, make you proud; some may frustrate you, while others may actually confuse you, but a true culturologist needs to learn to understand all aspects of your culture so that you can begin to create the needed culture to bring you into the future.

While I have spent time in numerous other countries and learned countless aspects of foreign culture, my learning is constantly in process. I am learning new things all of the time. As I learn new nuances of culture, I am that much more prepared to lead in culture engineering to help create a needed culture within my team so that we can be as ready as possible to not only encounter the future, but to create the future.

One of our staff, Lena, is finishing up her college degree. In Indonesia every student has a month long community service practicum where they go in groups of 8-10 students from different majors to live in a village and seek to help that village in whatever way they are able. Lena's teammates were shocked that she is already planning what's next in her life and has a very clear picture of what she desires to do. Long-term planning is not a part of Indonesian culture, but it is a part of our team's culture. Lena went on to help some of her teammates begin to think through possible and desirable futures for their lives as well as help lead her team to bring a bigger impact to the people in the village they were serving.

Another of our staff, Sius, is the youngest in his family, but now has the most varied background out of his entire family. He's been overseas, helped start a branch office, lived with foreigners, started neighborhood English chat clubs, has helped organize medical clinics for the poor in his home village, and oozes with passion for people. Whenever he goes home to his village (which I shared about earlier in *Culturology*), everyone wants his input. Even though he is the baby of the family, his training, experience, and different "culture" as a result of being on our staff has gained him the respect of an elder. In his home village, when Sius speaks, people listen.

Organizational culture should not only be about increasing the performance of your staff, but be about improving their lives and the lives of others. DeKluyver & Pearce (2009) state that, "Because of its pronounced effect on employee behavior and effectiveness, companies increasingly recognize that corporate culture can set them apart from competitors" (p. 43). To be set apart from our competitors we need to make steps and begin to be a culturologist; leaders who can understand our current organizational culture, our environment and market, and with the cooperation of our staff, begin to identify needed changes in our culture and take steps to bring change where it's needed.

Schein (2009) helps us to understand more of the role of a culturologist stating, "We need to develop our cultural intelligence; the culture leader of the future must be prepared to be more culturally intelligent – more motivated to understand others and more flexible in his or her own behavioral repertoire. Learning about culture requires effort. Once you have developed cultural intelligence you will be amazed how rewarding it is. You will find wisdom and an increased capacity to work with others whose thoughts and feelings may be very different than yours" (p. 224).

In the end, creating an organizational culture which will bring change in the lives of your staff and the life of your community (locally and globally) can only be successful as leaders begin to take culture learning seriously and begin to live as culturologists.

The winner of the 1957 Nobel Prize for Literature, Albert Camus, states that, "without culture, and the relative freedom it implies, society, even when perfect, is but a jungle. This is why any authentic creation is a gift to the future." Remember that you are not simply a leader, a boss, a CEO, a CFO, a manager, a staff member, or a founding partner by chance. You are designed to be a gift to the future and have been placed in your role of leadership to enable others in your organization to see that they are also designed to be a gift to the future. In the dense jungle of society, culturologists can help bring transformation from the inside out creating value not only to staff or shareholders, but to the entire world.

Do you believe in the power of one? Do you believe that you could be that one? The world sure hopes so. Many people around the world are desperately waiting for those who will be their advocates and voices of hope. There is no other step which will bring more fulfillment in your own life and the life of your staff than to live as a culturologist.

Discussion Questions

1. Is your organizational culture one that can allow you to win a big race, even against your best competitors? Better yet, could your staff win in your absence? Why or why not?

2. In terms of surfing, how are your key leaders and your organization doing riding the waves of the future? What could you do to increase the speed of your reactions to changes?

3. How can a change in organizational culture, climate, and value of people in your context translate into helping the world?

4. What are some things your organization is uniquely gifted to do in helping the world become a better place?

5. Have you ever considered someone (a paid staff position) to be involved in community (local and global) outreach and humanitarian projects? Why or why not? What's stopping you?

6. List out three things your organization could do in the next year locally, nationally, and internationally to help people, groups of people, villages, cities, governments, or nations (remember the more hands on the better). Who will be in charge of helping make this happen?

   Local:

      a. _____

         _____

b. _____

_____

c. _____

_____

National:

a. _____

_____

b. _____

_____

c. _____

_____

International:

a. _____

_____

b. _____

_____

c. _____

_____

7. What changes do you have to make to become a culturologist? Do you believe in the power of one? Or could I say the power of "you"? Use this space to write out goals you have to begin to bring needed change to your organization as well as people you need to recruit to help you do it.

FREE DOWNLOAD

Take advantage of the free download at **www.culturologybook.com** These are the questions at the end of each chapter put into a discussion book format so that your team can have room to write our their answers, questions, and brainstorm together so that you can get the most out of *Culturology* and create the best culture for sustainable growth.

What's underneath impacts everything!

www.culturologybook.com

References

Adamchik, W. (2006). *No Yelling: The 9 Secrets of Marine Corps Leadership You Must Know to Win in Business*. Raleigh, NC: Firestarter.

Aziza, B. & Fitts, J. (2008). *Drive Business Performance: Enabling a Culture of Intelligent Execution*. Hoboken, NJ: John Wiley & Sons, Inc.

Biehl, B. (2008). *Masterplanning: The Complete Guide for Building a Strategic Plan for your Business, Church, or Organization*. Mt. Dora, FL: Aylen Publishing.

Bradford, R. W. & Duncan, J. P. (2000). *Simplified Strategic Planning*. Worcester, MA: Chandler House Press.

Cameron, K. S. & Quinn, R. E. (2006). *Diagnosing and changing Organizational Culture*. San Francisco, CA: Jossey-Bass.

Canton, J. (2006). *The Extreme Future*. New York, NY: Dutton.

Collins, J. (2001). *Good to Great: Why Some Companies Make the Leap...and Others Don't*. New York, NY: Harper Business.

Cornish, E. (2004). *Futuring: The Exploration of the*

Future. Bethesda, MD: World Future Society.

Crouch, A. (2008). *Culture Making: Recovering Our Creative Calling.* Downers Grover, IL: InterVarsity Press.

Daft, R. L. (2008). *The Leadership Experience.* Mason, OH: Thomson/South-Western.

DeKluyver, C. A. & Pearce III, J. A. (2009). *Strategy: A View from the Top.* Upper Saddle River, NJ: Pearson Education.

Driskill, G.W. & Brenton, A. L. (2011). *Organizational Culture in Action: A Cultural Analysis Workbook.* Los Angeles, CA: Sage.

Eikenberry, K. (n.d.). *Seven Reasons Organizational Culture Matters.* Ezinearticles. Retrieved on January 4, 2011 from http://ezinearticles.com/?Seven-Reasons-Organizational-Culture-Matters&id=164337

Eikenberry, K. (n.d.). Seven Ways to Enhance Organizational Culture. Business Performance. Retrieved on January 4, 2011 from http://www.businessperform.com/articles/organizational-culture/enhance_organizational_culture.html

Frost, P. J., Moore, L. F., Louis, M. R., Lundberg, C. C. & Martin, J. (Eds.). (1991). *Reframing*

Organizational Culture. Newbury Park, CA: Sage Publications.

Gladwell, M. (2002). *The Tipping Point: How Little Things Can Make a Big Difference*. New York, NY: Little, Brown and Company.

Goodin, S. (2002). *Purple Cow: Transform Your Business by Being Remarkable*. New York, NY: Penguin Books.

Harrison, R. & Stokes, H. (1992). *Diagnosing Organizational Culture*. San Francisco, CA: Jossey-Bass.

Harvard Business Review. (2002). *Culture and Change*. Boston, MA: Harvard Business Review.

Hines, A. & Bishop, P. (eds.) (2006). *Thinking about the Future: Guidelines for Strategic Growth*. Washington, DC: Social Technologies.

Hughes, R. L. & Beatty, K. C. (2005). *Becoming a Strategic Leader: Your Role in Your Organization's Enduring Success*. San Francisco, CA: Jossey-Bass.

Littlejohn, S. W. & Foss, K. A. (2008). *Theories of Human Communication*. Belmont, CA: Thomson Higher Education.

Kotelnikov, V. (2011). Corporate Culture. Achieving higher results through sustaining employees'

focus on what to do and how to do it. E-Coach
Website. Retrieved on January 05, 2011 from
http://www/1000venture.com/business_guide/
crosscuttings/culture_corporate.html

Michel, A. & Wortham, S. (2009). *Bullish on
Uncertainty: How Organizational Cultures
Transform Participants*. New York: NY:
Cambridge University Press.

Muller, R. (2001). *Honor and Shame.* Bloomington,
IN: Xlibris.

Nanus, B. (1992). *Visionary Leadership*. San
Francisco, CA: Jossey-Bass.

Ralston, B. & Wilson, I. (2006). *The Scenario
Planning Handbook: Developing Strategies in
Uncertain Times.* Mason, OH: Thomson/South-
Western.

Samuel, M. S. (n.d.). The Direct Link Between
Business Results and Organizational Culture.
Ezinearticles. Retrieved on January 4, 2011 from
http://ezinearticles.com/?The-Direct-Link-
Between-Business-Results-and-Organizational-
Culture&id=4723304

Sanders, J. O. (2007). *Spiritual Leadership*.
Chicago, IL: Moody Publishers.

Schein, E. H. (2010). *Organizational Culture and*

Leadership. San Francisco, CA: Jossey-Bass.

Schein, E. H. (2009). *The Corporate Culture Survival Guide*. San Francisco, CA: Jossey-Bass.

Schein, E. H. (1992). *Organizational Culture and Leadership* (2nd ed.). San Francisco, CA: Jossey-Bass.

Scott, C. D., Jaffe, D. T. & Tobe, G, R. (1993). *Organizational Vision, Values, and Mission: Building the Organization of Tomorrow*. Menlo Park, CA: Crisp Publications, Inc.

Senge, P. M. (2006). *The Fifth Discipline: The Art & Practice of the Learning Organization*. New York, NY: Currency.

Shockley-Zalabak, P. S. (2009). *Fundamentals of Organizational Communication: Knowledge, Sensitivity, Skills, Values*. New York, NY: Pearson Education.

www.ingramcontent.com/pod-product-compliance
Lightning Source LLC
Chambersburg PA
CBHW031951170526
45157CB00002B/452